P9-CQU-421

Mary L. Gray

In Your Face
Stories from the Lives of Queer Youth

Pre-publication REVIEWS, COMMENTARIES, EVALUATIONS . . .

"*In Your Face* takes its place in the small but growing body of work that gives a real voice to sexual-minority youth. It is refreshing that the academic analysis takes a backseat to the narratives of the youth who have come forward to share their lives. Rather than focusing on victimization, suicide, and the other horrors associated with sexual-minority youth, this book provides a holistic view of their lives with all the variability that entails—the good and the bad, the ups and the downs. It reminds us that queer youth are real people with complex lives and relationships that cannot be reduced to a linear model of the coming-out process. These youth come from a variety of backgrounds—ethnically, geographically, and socioeconomically. And rather than offering a template for their interactions with family, friends, schools, and communities, these narratives celebrate the diversity of experiences of sexual-minority youth. The book puts a multiplicity of faces on the category of queer youth."

Margaret Schneider, PhD
Associate Professor,
University of Toronto

More pre-publication
REVIEWS, COMMENTARIES, EVALUATIONS . . .

"*In Your Face: Stories from the Lives of Queer Youth* by Mary L. Gray is a valuable addition to the literature documenting the lives of sexual-minority youth. It will be most appreciated by youth as they read about the lives of fifteen who came before them—a group of diverse teens who have faced and resolved to varying degrees the dilemmas of growing up with same-sex attractions.

But this book is not just for kids—it is also for the rest of us who celebrate the lives of queer youth. Their stories will move us beyond our own historically and culturally insular experiences as we listen to their wisdoms, successes, and failures. Gray wants this book to fill the void of voice and testimony from youth talking about their queer sexuality and identity so that we, as adults, will be prepared to ask sexual-minority youth *real* questions and listen to their *real* answers.

This book belongs to the genre of coming-out stories, but with a difference. It comprises uninterrupted and undigested life accounts. Each youth takes a turn answering questions about self-labeling his or her sexual identity; coming out to family and friends; confronting societal institutions such as religion and school; becoming involved in lesbian/bi/gay communities and the Internet; and being sexual. Because of my particular academic and clinical focus, I was most interested in Chapter 3, as it well represents the diversity of experiences disclosing to parents and the range of parental reactions. My favorite material was the youths' responses to the question: 'What would you like to say to folks out there—young or old, straight and queer?' Their answers are insightful, funny, sad, and angry, and are from youth who have embraced life and want other queer youth to do the same."

Ritch C. Savin-Williams
Professor of Developmental and Clinical Psychology, Cornell University, Ithaca, NY

The Haworth Press, Inc.

NOTES FOR PROFESSIONAL LIBRARIANS AND LIBRARY USERS

This is an original book title published by The Haworth Press, Inc. Unless otherwise noted in specific chapters with attribution, materials in this book have not been previously published elsewhere in any format or language.

CONSERVATION AND PRESERVATION NOTES

All books published by The Haworth Press, Inc. and its imprints are printed on certified pH neutral, acid free book grade paper. This paper meets the minimum requirements of American National Standard for Information Sciences–Permanence of Paper for Printed Material, ANSI Z39.48-1984.

In Your Face
Stories from the Lives of Queer Youth

HAWORTH Gay & Lesbian Studies
John P. De Cecco, PhD
Editor in Chief

The Bear Book: Readings in the History and Evolution of a Gay Male Subculture edited by Les Wright

Youths Living with HIV: Self-Evident Truths by G. Cajetan Luna

Growth and Intimacy for Gay Men: A Workbook by Christopher J. Alexander

Our Families, Our Values: Snapshots of Queer Kinship edited by Robert E. Goss and Amy Adams Squire Strongheart

Gay/Lesbian/Bisexual/Transgender Public Policy Issues: A Citizen's and Administrator's Guide to the New Cultural Struggle edited by Wallace Swan

Rough News, Daring Views: 1950s' Pioneer Gay Press Journalism by Jim Kepner

Family Secrets: Gay Sons—A Mother's Story by Jean M. Baker

Twenty Million New Customers: Understanding Gay Men's Consumer Behavior by Steven M. Kates

The Empress Is a Man: Stories from the Life of José Sarria by Michael R. Gorman

Acts of Disclosure: The Coming-Out Process of Contemporary Gay Men by Marc E. Vargo

Queer Kids: The Challenges and Promise for Lesbian, Gay, and Bisexual Youth by Robert E. Owens

Looking Queer: Body Image and Identity in Lesbian, Gay, Bisexual, and Transgender Communities edited by Dawn Atkins

Love and Anger: Essays on AIDS, Activism, and Politics by Peter F. Cohen

Dry Bones Breathe: Gay Men Creating Post-AIDS Identities and Cultures by Eric Rofes

Lila's House: Male Prostitution in Latin America by Jacobo Schifter

A Consumer's Guide to Male Hustlers by Joseph Itiel

Trailblazers: Profiles of America's Gay and Lesbian Elected Officials by Kenneth E. Yeager

Rarely Pure and Never Simple: Selected Essays by Scott O'Hara

Navigating Differences: Friendships Between Gay and Straight Men by Jammie Price

In the Pink: The Making of Successful Gay- and Lesbian-Owned Businesses by Sue Levin

Behold the Man: The Hype and Selling of Male Beauty in Media and Culture by Edisol Wayne Dotson

Untold Millions: Secret Truths About Marketing to Gay and Lesbian Consumers by Grant Lukenbill

It's a Queer World: Deviant Adventures in Pop Culture by Mark Simpson

In Your Face: Stories from the Lives of Queer Youth by Mary L. Gray

Military Trade by Steven Zeeland

Longtime Companions: Autobiographies of Gay Male Fidelity by Alfred Lees and Ronald Nelson

From Toads to Queens: Transvestism in a Latin American Setting by Jacobo Schifter

The Construction of Attitudes Toward Lesbians and Gay Men by Lynn Pardie and Tracy Luchetta

Lesbian Epiphanies: Women Coming Out in Later Life by Karol L. Jensen

In Your Face
Stories from the Lives of Queer Youth

Mary L. Gray

The Haworth Press
New York • London • Oxford

The Haworth Press, Inc., 10 Alice Street, Binghamton, NY 13904-1580

Cover design by Monica L. Seifert.

Library of Congress Cataloging-in-Publication Data

Gray, Mary L.
In your face : stories from the lives of queer youth / Mary L. Gray.
p. cm.
ISBN 0-7890-0076-8 (alk. paper).
1. Gay youth—United States. 2. Homosexuality—United States. I. Title.
HQ76.3.U5G73 1999
305.235—dc21 98-46426
CIP

I dedicate this book to Andrew Brosnan, my dear friend, research assistant, pizza delivery boy, spell checker, and copy editor extraordinaire. Thank you, Andrew. I wrote this for you as much as I wrote it for myself.

ABOUT THE AUTHOR

Mary L. Gray is a doctoral candidate in Communication at the University of California at San Diego. A queer youth rights advocate and activist, she co-moderates the only on-line support newsgroup for queer youth and continues to act as a consultant to agencies using new media technologies for political and social activism.

CONTENTS

Acknowledgments

This collection was very much a collaborative project. The fifteen people whose stories you are about to read (as well as any youth I met while researching queer identity who are not included in this collection) all contributed to the making of this book. They are more accurately co-authors of this project, for without our shared commitment to publish stories for both other youth and adult allies to read, there would be nothing new for me to tell you.

I want to personally thank: Paige, Lisa Campbell, Eriq Chang, Eileene Coscolluela, Anthony Gomez, Jim, Adam Hardy, Ernie Hsiung, Mathis, Todd Fay-Long, Dawn McCausland, Kyallee Santanders, Michael Talis, Mary Toth, and Alan Wiley. They are an opinionated and proud bunch. I apologize to them for having taken so long to get their words of wisdom out, but hope they will take satisfaction in seeing the impact their comments will make on a generation of youth like themselves.

I also want to thank my editor, mentor, and greatest supporter, John De Cecco, as well as The Haworth Press, for having the faith in this project to support it through both time and grants. The transcription work of Barbara Smith was invaluable, of course; she managed to catch every "uh" and "like" uttered, which in itself is amazing. My family—big sister, Verda, mom, and "pops"—have all bragged enough about me that I felt the needed extra pressure to actually finish this book to live up to their boasting. I have leaned heavily on my partner in crime, Mary T., and many of my friends, and I missed many group gatherings because of this project; everyone's patience, particularly that of the Davis gang (you all know who you are), has been greatly appreciated.

Introduction

Why Do We Need Books Like This?

The lack of firsthand accounts from young people identifying as lesbian, gay, bi, and transgendered is not coincidental. The radical right works diligently to drive queer teachers from the classroom, pushing the panic button for fear that these teachers will "recruit" unsuspecting (presumedly) straight students; in response, a fearful adult queer community builds distance between itself and youth, particularly those questioning their sexuality; add to this our society's ever-present attitude that the experiences of youth are less than real. Combined homophobia and ageism, fixtures of our social landscape, have effectively rendered the realities of lesbian, gay, bi, and transgendered young people invisible to both the queer and straight worlds.

In most cases, people's views on homosexuality reflect the beliefs and values of their communities. One cannot deny that the current attitudes about queer sexuality are less than supportive and positive. Consider, then, the experience of a young person in an average family in which the parents hold the average views on homosexuality. Also, imagine the teachers and fellow students in such an environment. The young person coming out will likely feel relatively unsafe in his or her home and classes; he or she will probably be exposed to the everyday forms of humiliation, hearing "fag" jokes and derogatory language, without anyone ever considering that such comments may actually be hurtful to others. The only other people who may be sympathetic are other adults or youth who understand coming out firsthand.

However, a young person's coming-out process can tap a queer adult's own painful buried memories of dealing with queerness, triggering the adult's paranoia that he or she will be blamed for the young person's exploration of a queer identity. Identifying other questioning youth in such unsafe territories as school halls and neighborhoods can be next to impossible. It often feels as if you can't risk talking with anyone because the cost of guessing wrong about who to approach is too high.

Even in cases in which adults, queer or straight, can accept the young person's choice to explore sexuality, often the young person's conclusions about his or her identity will be met with such responses as, "You're too young to really know," or a doubting, "Are you sure?"—As if we ever, in adulthood particularly, know anything for sure.

Our society does not ask questions of its youth because it does not expect to get a "real" answer: to ask youth questions is to ask for a half-baked truth, one still in formation and yet to be definitively shaped. Our society does not expect that youth can possibly know who they are or what they want. Young people are left without affirming support from anyone, queer or straight. The message to youth from all sides is that what they think they may be is wrong and bad and ugly, and definitely not something to embrace.

The motivation, then, to create this book came from the complete absence of voice and testimony from youth talking about their queer sexuality and identity, the result of society's homophobia and its ever-present ageist sensibilities of whose view counts.

Several psychological studies have been conducted with adults who were recalling the first signs of their sexuality or reflecting on their own coming-out processes. The work of psychologist Ritch Savin-Williams on youth suicide is particularly significant for its commitment to surveying youth rather than relying on data from secondary sources such as school psychologists or other health professionals working with youth. Unfortunately, most studies along these lines become quickly outdated because society's ways of dealing with queer sexuality change rapidly.

Since beginning this project, a handful of books have been added to the growing body of literature on queer youth (see Herdt and Boxer's *Children of Horizons*, Rofes's *Reviving the Tribe*, and *The Gay Teen* by Unks for examples). *Joining the Tribe* by journalist Linna Due makes a groundbreaking contribution by actually focusing on first-person accounts from queer youth talking about their lives. However, with the exception of the landmark pieces *One Teenager in Ten* and *Two Teen-*

agers in Twenty, edited by Ann Heron, no oral histories have been taken from anyone queer under the age of eighteen.

Something truly revolutionary is happening—more young people (both in the United States and elsewhere) are rejecting a heterosexual norm at earlier and earlier ages. Fifteen years ago, it would have been difficult, even next to impossible, for me to find anyone eighteen years old or younger to talk about coming out. Young people were not talking about being queer; they were, more often than not, deeply in the closet, with no affirming (let alone peer-driven) resources available to discuss their identities.

Now, at almost exponential rates, high schools are forming (or fighting the formation of) Gay/Straight Alliance groups and coming-out discussion groups for thirteen- to sixteen-year-olds and sixteen- to eighteen-year-olds. This is an incredible and complex shift. We are unlikely to understand what changes to our cultural, social, and political climate this represents without taking the opportunity to speak with the young people who are both directly impacted by and actively affecting these rapid metamorphoses.

And, in very real terms, the more we come to understand, the better we can prevent youth from contemplating suicide just because they think they may be lesbian, gay, bisexual, or transgendered. (In the United States the suicide rate for queer youth is three times the national average for all youth.)

Having now presented some of the motivations behind this project, I want to mention a few details about the process behind gathering the stories, in addition to comments on what is missing from this book.

What started out as my thesis work in anthropology—seeking to understand what "queer" identity means to young people in the late 1990s—has become a venue for youth to speak for themselves about their lives.

I mailed flyers to queer youth support groups around the San Francisco Bay Area calling for interview volunteers and went to several open group meetings to let folks know about the project and my intent. The most I could offer people was a free lunch and the hope that their stories would reach others like them.

Many of the stories are transcriptions of taped sessions in which the participants came together on a single day, paired up and interviewed one another. I used this method because I thought it would be much more interesting and effective to have young people asking one another the questions—to break out of the traditional social science methodologies of anonymously interviewing numbered subjects.

Once together, the group discussed what topics would be most important to cover. Everyone agreed that certain issues were key: coming out to oneself, family, and friends; school environments; involvement with the queer adult community; and the impact of religion on one's sense of self. I added the suggestion that people discuss their relationships, some general background (age, where they grew up, and what that was like), and what plans they had for their futures, ending with messages they would want to pass on to others.

You will also find here a few stories that came from chat sessions and e-mail exchanges with people who participated in this project via the Internet. We started with the questions brought up in the previously described first interview session and let the conversation move on from there.

I was particularly interested in (and continue to explore) the impact the Internet has on identity among youth coming out in places that do not have "off-line" communities of support. I wanted to know if youth in rural areas, places not unlike my own hometown of Clovis in central California, were using the Net to find out what it means to be gay/lesbian/bi/transgendered. I am now examining how this process is affecting the face of the queer movement globally, as more people, younger and younger, begin to deal with their sexuality in increasingly public ways (forming support groups of their own on-line, becoming the editors of on-line queer youth 'zines, or just finding dates in chat rooms).

The structure of this book allows readers to learn some background about each of the speakers. Each of the book's chapters focuses on a different subject so that readers can choose what they wish to read about and see the varying experiences each speaker has with that particular topic. The intent was to show that not all queer youth have the same experiences or feelings on subjects central or common to their lives. This book's format also enables readers to find a particular person's stories quickly and easily in each chapter, without having to scan the entire book for their favorite person or the one with whom they identify the most.

Conspicuously absent from this collection are the voices of transgendered youth. I initially tried to find youth under eighteen who identified as transgendered. My attempts were unsuccessful, and I had limited resources and time available to work with the collected material. In hindsight, I wish I had continued to seek out young people who could provide a transgendered perspective.

The issues faced by transgendered youth have only recently come to the surface, shockingly exemplified by cases such as that of Brandon Teena, a teenage female-to-male transsexual who was brutally raped and murdered by a group of vengeful young straight men, as well as the continued reported abuses of "gender identity disorder" diagnoses by doctors and parents seeking to "straighten out" their children (see artist Daphne Scholinksi's chilling accounts in her autobiography, *Last Time I Wore a Dress.*)

The intersections of gender and sexual identity are complex and have received little investigation. Any hopes we have of working through these complexities rest in our ability to seek out the experiences and voices of those living through the confused crossfire of society's (mis)understandings of what transgendered identity means. We must also work with these youth to redefine "transgendered" in the coming decade.

Also conspicuous is my use of the term queer to describe the youth in this collection. For convenience and because of my own political identity as a queer woman, I use queer to collectively refer to people identifying as lesbian, bisexual, transgendered, or gay. Queer can be a very loaded term and I do not wish to make light of it, particularly since several of the youth in this collection actively reject the word queer as a term of self-reference. No single term of self-reference was used by all youth involved, and, in fact, they called themselves everything from "freak" and "fag" to "dyke" and "your plain old garden-variety homosexual." That was simply too many identities to put in the title of a book, so I chose "queer" to capture it all. It is not my intention to offend, only to abbreviate and simplify. I make no other attempts to impose my language upon the speakers here and hope no one will take offense to the word.

Chapter 1

Background: Profiles of the People You Will Meet in This Book

NOTES ON WHO YOU WILL HEAR IN THIS COLLECTION

The young people in this collection are a diverse group with a range of experiences, classes, ethnicities, and sexual identities. The stories of fifteen speakers—nine young men and six young women—ranging in ages from fourteen to eighteen, are presented here.

This first chapter attempts to contextualize the voices behind the stories you are about to read, by providing the backgrounds of the young people in this collection. In chronicling the stories of their family lives, hometowns, and general life circumstances at the time they were interviewed, I hoped to document something timeless: where they were at and where they had been.

These backdrops—the finer points of their histories and biographies—may shift in perspective with the passage of time, but they are relatively stable, physical pictures. Learning you are not the only queer person in the world takes on even greater meaning when you discover that there are also others out there from similar cultures, classes, or family dynamics. This contextualization—often left out of similar studies—provides additional points of recognition and resonance for the reader.

I find it striking that so many of the youth in this collection, regardless of their backgrounds, express, at very early ages, a sense of isolation and desire for connection. The sentiment of "feeling different" can be interpreted in many ways. Some see this commonality of expression as evidence for a genetic link to sexual orientation. Others may read this as the connection felt among those who have endured the same oppression. However, many young people brought up in the fractured and disjointed atmosphere of U.S. capitalist consumption may express a similar sense of isolation regardless of their sexual identity. What makes these young people different from their heterosexual peers?

Unique to this group is that they have sought loving connections beyond the heterosexual norm, and they choose to view these desires as defining characteristics of who they are. And in pursuing these relationships, they face a common obstruction to these desires: a predominantly hostile, unaccepting, and homophobic social environment.

Their backgrounds illustrate that they are not dramatically different from other young people you may encounter in the United States today. They come from a broad base of circumstances that are relatively unremarkable and arguably typical (of course, defining typical is a highly contestable enterprise). Yet they are hardly just like everyone else their age. They endure a discrimination that permeates practically every social sphere of their lives, from their communities and churches to their schools and often, sadly, their homes.

The young people included in this collection are in no way meant to represent all youth identifying as gay, lesbian, or bisexual. But, hopefully, the people here will cast reflections of youth the reader knows or identifies with in some way. The examples of resiliency depicted demonstrate various strategies implemented by queer youth to establish and fortify their identities. Although the juxtaposition of their stories reveals how different the lives of gay, lesbian, and bi youth can be, it also illustrates how much they share in common as a result of the adversity they have faced in a homophobic society.

* * *

Anthony Gomez

My name is Anthony Gomez. I'm a fourteen-year-old gay male. My birth date is May 3rd. I was born and raised in Healdsburg, California. It's a redneck town. Right now, my space of living is Hayward in a group home. I call it home/hell, same thing. My six housemates are assholes.

My father is in Arizona State Prison. I haven't had any connection with him for about ten years. And all of a sudden, I get letters from him now every so often. He says he misses me. I would like to be able to have something with my father and have him be there for me. The thing is, he does not know I'm homosexual. And I know I'm afraid of telling him. I want to tell him face to face. And I'm afraid if I don't, he'll run away. It took so long to find him. I went to Arizona four times before I finally found him.

I have two sisters and one brother. They're all little. One is three-and-a-half years old, the other one is two-and-a-half, and the other one is around eight months. I have two stepsisters who are eighteen and sixteen, and one fourteen-year-old stepbrother. I'm like the black sheep because I'm just out there, but I didn't tell them I was gay myself. I never really had the nerve to tell them. The night they found out I was gay was the night that I got taken to a mental hospital, and then from there, I was placed in a group home. So, I never got their reaction. Me and my mom got in a fight that night and I said, "I'm better off dead . . . . You don't care about me; I don't give a damn if you come to this house right now and kill me." She called the police, 'cause we were having this huge argument. And so my mom told the police what I said, and they took me. Well, right now I'm trying to get out of the group home. I need a place where I can be stable—where I can actually sort out my problems, without all the bullshit that goes on in the house.

Adam Hardy

My name is Adam Hardy. I'm now eighteen years old; I'm from Huntsville, Alabama, and I go to college at Simon's Rock College of Bard in Great Barrington, Massachusetts. That, in itself, doesn't tell you much about me. However, the story might become interesting if I told you that I was a high school dropout; that I went to college early; that I dropped out of my senior year because of the serious homophobia in my old high school that was killing me.

Not that Huntsville was such an awful place to live. I miss it terribly sometimes. The city is actually rather northern, since Redstone Arsenal, Intergraph, and a few major companies draw in people from all over the nation to live in the city. That's probably why I don't have a southern accent. However, the subtext to the city is *entirely* southern and shapes a lot of the attitudes that people have about religion, abortion, and homosexuality. I'd say Huntsville is a pretty large city, one of the major ones in Alabama. I lived there until a little over a year ago. Right now, I'm finishing up my first semester as a sophomore here at college.

I grew up being the closest thing going to an only child—my sister Katie was eleven years older than I and moved out when I was six or seven. My parents are typically dysfunctional, and my mother went through a lot of changes when she had me. She'd "failed" at parenting with one child—she's always been rather strict with Katie and submissive to my father—and she was determined to be as "present" a parent as possible. She was sick and bedridden for most of my childhood, and I spent a lot of my time with her, playing games and learning to love reading and drawing.

My father was night to my mother's day. My mom is warm, giving, emotional, extremely liberal, and she's loved me unconditionally all my life. My father seems to have shut down emotionally at some point. He's cold, inexpressive, repressed, and is really only capable of showing anger and frustration. His sense of humor disturbs me, as he only laughs when others are embarrassed or in pain. My father was sort of the mold for my personality, as the plaster fitted onto someone's face is the template for a bust . . . I was determined to be everything he wasn't. I suppose that this makes me a prime target for conservatives who believe that homosexuality is caused by having a weak father figure and a strong maternal figure. The way I see it, I had less of a masculine role to rebel against when I came out to myself, facilitating that process. My father is, of course, hopelessly conservative.

My family, beyond the immediate, consists of my mother's side, who I will tolerate, and my father's side, whom I will not. My father's side is mostly made up of very conservative people; my mother's side is made up of mostly dead people. One is much easier for me to deal with than the other. I care for my grandmother, but wouldn't much notice if most of the rest of the family were to suddenly up and vanish.

Alan Wiley

My name is Alan Wiley, and I'm eighteen. I was born on November 19th in Bellflower, California. I lived in Costa Mesa until I was two years old, and then I moved to Poway, California, where I lived until I went away to school to San Francisco State. I've got one younger brother who's seventeen and one older sister who's twenty-one. My parents are still married, and I usually live with both of them when I'm not at school. My mother is a priest, and my father is an elder and has been a minister and pastor in the Reorganized Church of Jesus Christ of Latter-Day Saints, or the RLDS church.

Poway is suburban hell. It's a really extremely Mormon, extremely Christian town. It probably has maybe 60 to 80,000 people in it. I lived there for a long time, pretty much my whole life all my life that I can remember. It's very conservative, and I had a really difficult time dealing with my sexuality because of that.

Eileene Coscolluela

I'm nineteen, and my birthday is July 11th. Nutley, New Jersey, is my hometown. It's a very small, conservative town—well, small in comparison to other towns in the area. It's a suburb of New York City. The high school has fewer than 1,000 students (my graduating class is about 220). My town has primarily forty-year-olds and older. The crime rate is exceptionally low, and the average income in the town ranges from the extremely affluent to lower middle class. I've lived in the town since 1979, when I first came into the country from the Philippines. I have a younger sister who's thirteen years old. I have a mother and a father. My uncle, my mother's brother, is currently living with us, a recent immigrant from the Philippines.

Dawn McCausland

My name is Dawn McCausland, my age is seventeen, and my birth date is April 21st, which means next month I'll be eighteen. I grew up in Sebastopol, California, which is in Sonoma County; it's kind of country, fairly liberal, and not a very culturally diverse area. It was a pretty good place to grow up.

My father passed away when I was four months old. I grew up with a stepfather, a stepbrother, my sister, and my mother. My parents were both psychologists when I was growing up. My mother went back to school through all my growing years. Then my parents got divorced, and I lived with my mother. It was around that time, after the divorce, that I started dealing with coming-out issues. That was the beginning of high school; I was about fourteen.

Eriq Chang

I was born in Walnut Creek, California, and I moved to Pleasanton, California. Pleasanton is a pretty conservative town. It's considered a rich city. But that's about it. I'm seventeen. I live with my parents. I have one sister. My sister knows that I am bisexual, and my parents do not. My sister is fourteen. We do a lot of things together. I do drag—just sort of a fun thing. So, she kinda knows; she asked, and I didn't want to lie to her. I turn eighteen November 20th. I'm a Sagittarius. I think it's just gonna be, "I'm eighteen." I've done a lot of things at this age that even people who are twenty haven't done. I don't drink. I don't see any point in going on about drinking and stuff. So age, for me, hasn't been a big, total setback or advantage. I've been able to accomplish a lot of things at this age, which is really cool. Jogging is my passion. I have to jog. It's The Thing. If I don't jog, I get depressed. And I've been depressed this week.

I've been taking pictures for about six, seven years. I got really good at it two years ago because I studied Annie Liebowitz and Tom Bianchi. I totally study their work. I love art. I really do. That's what makes the world go 'round, which is probably why I like taking pictures of things.

I love pop music—I really love dance music. Dance music is the release for me. That's how I can vent my frustrations at times, just totally dance and go off. I love Dee Lite. I used to like C&C, but now they're gone. The mix master, I'd have to say, is Junior Vasquez, who remade "Secret." I love Tori Amos. She's so-o-o rad. She's like a goddess, I think.

Ernie Hsiung

I am eighteen years old. I was born in Hayward, California and raised in El Sobrante, Califonia, a small suburb a couple of minutes from Berkeley. I lived there ever since junior high (seventh grade.) I live with two parents and a sister. My father is currently sixty-two, my mother fifty-nine. My sister is twenty-eight, ten years older than I am. Since my sister is so old, I consider her more of a mother than anything else. It was difficult living with my sister because I had to live with her through her hardships. She has a learning disability. She had a mental breakdown at fifteen. (I still remember the police dragging her out of the house when I was five.) I saw her life as she became dependent on medication, how she "gave her life to Christ," how she now lives by herself in a rented room, barely making it month to month. Being Chinese, this puts a lot of pressure on me to succeed.

Since I am a first generation Chinese American, I was raised speaking English, while my parents speak to me in Chinese. (My mother to this day refuses to speak to me in English.) This causes a lot of communication problems. While I can talk to my parents about conventional things—dinner, money for college, the weather outside—I am unable to talk to them about abstract ideas, such as my being gay, without added bits of fractured English.

Kyallee Santanders

I'm nineteen years old; I was born April 22nd. Most of my schooling took place in Falcon, Colorado. My parents lived in nearby Black Forest. My high school had 500 kids in it, and the school was literally in the middle of a cow pasture. In other words, it was pretty rural. . . . I moved there at age ten and stayed there until I "escaped" to Boulder at eighteen.

Growing up in Falcon, I was living with my parents and four younger siblings. I now live in the engineering dorms in my own room. The roommate thing just never seemed to work out—they'd claim to be open-minded, but then they'd go tell all of their friends what saints they were for living with a lesbian.

Lisa Campbell

My name is Lisa Campbell. I'm eighteen years old; my birth date is March 11th. I'm originally from Louisiana. I lived in two different towns; Sugartown, and Merryville, on the Texas border near the Sabine River, in Beauregard Parish. You probably have no idea where that's at. The biggest town near there is Leesville, and then Lake Charles is probably a hundred miles or something from there. I lived in Louisiana for about twelve years—so basically from the time I was about two 'til the time I was about eleven.

Sugartown was very small, a couple thousand people. At our high school, there's maybe a thousand people, and that's counting preschool to twelfth. It's a working town. Most of the people in the towns that I lived in were doing factory jobs at a place called Boise Cascade. People like my mom had jobs at the sewing factory and local grocery stores and stuff like that—people trying to get by. It was a poor town basically. I can't go back there and live a straight life.

I have one half brother, and, well, before my mom got divorced, I had two stepbrothers growing up. They were around pretty much the whole time I was growing up. One was my age and one was about three years older than I. The one my age and I argued all the time; we were stuck in the same class two years in a row. The teachers sat us right across from each other.

January of last year, my mom decided she wanted to get a divorce. And then it was finalized after my grandfather's death. It's weird now when I go back there because I don't see them, and if I do, we don't talk or anything.

I decided to move out of my mom's house after my fifth-grade year, and move to California and lived with my dad in Hercules, near the Richmond area. My mom didn't object because she knew her financial situation and everything, and things were gonna be pretty tight in the next year. I moved to California for a year, and then I decided that I wanted to go back to Louisiana. So I went back and I lived there for two years.

When I moved out I was eleven; I came back there when I was twelve. I had a job in the store where my mom worked for a while, I worked in the meat market packing meat, dealing with all the saws and the big meat grinder for ground meat and all that stuff.

I finished high school out here in California. Me and my mom were really clashing heads. Part of it was that she treated my half brother Richard, a lot differently than she treated me. I think some of it had to do with the fact that she was in love with Richard's father and she hates my father. I have a lot of characteristics that are like my father's: my hands, the way I look a lot of it is like my father. I can't help that. My mom just saw that my temperament and my personality were a lot like my father's, and she just couldn't live with that; she couldn't deal with it then.

My mom treated me pretty badly a lot of the time. She was going through some tough times, though, too. After I moved back there, Stanley, my stepfather, lost the house in a bad business deal, and they auctioned it off in the sheriff's auction; we ended up moving into town and renting a place for a while. The next year, in the summer, I went to see my dad; the day I came back and stepped off the plane, my mom said, "Don't unpack your suitcase tonight." The next day we moved out. It was three days before school started.

Because the towns I lived in were spread far apart, I had to change schools. It was an hour-and-a-half drive between each. I was supposed to be in the marching band that year, but I didn't get to do it because of that. A couple of years later, I was back with my dad.

Mathis

My name is Mathis. I'm eighteen. I was born August 30th in Phoenix, Arizona. I was raised primarily in the town of Pawnee, Oklahoma. I moved there in third grade, and I stayed there 'til tenth grade. Before that, in kindergarten, I was in Oklahoma and, after kindergarten, moved to New Mexico for two years and then moved back to Oklahoma. I went to several schools in Oklahoma, and then we finally settled in Pawnee.

I think Pawnee is about probably fifty-six miles from Tulsa. There were about 20,000 people there. The people were very uncommunity-like. They didn't have that much to do with one another; they always gossiped behind one another's backs and stuff. I was probably the most talked about person in town. Everybody knew who I was before I even knew who the hell they were. But I lived there with my mom and my mother's boyfriend, whom she got together with when I was five; she is still with him. My mom doesn't know who my father is.

Now I live in California with one of my uncles who was pretty much abandoned by my grandmother when he was little. I live with him and his family now. Right now the situation is very unusual because they think I'm too active in the gay lifestyle and the gay culture. They don't think I should be as out as I am. I'm not sure if it's necessarily what all the neighbors think or whether it's for my own protection. They think the world is just a horrible place and that I'm gonna go through hell. I try to explain to them I've already been through hell and I know what it's like, so I can deal with it. They don't understand that. I've decided to move out of my aunt's and uncle's house. I cannot stay there anymore because they aren't dealing with me well. I don't like to put a bind on them, and it's really putting some pressure on me. So it's like I'm all alone now, but I have my friends. My friends are very supportive. Actually, I don't know what I would do if I hadn't found them.

Michael Talis

I'm fifteen years old, born September 5th. I was born at Pennsylvania Hospital in Philadelphia, Pennsylvania. I have lived all over southeastern Pennsylvania. To explain why I moved and where, you have to understand my parental situation, so I'll weave that in. My parents got divorced, and so starts my moving career. I was with my mom for the most part and saw my dad on weekends. Both of my parents stayed in Center City, Philadelphia, for a while, though living separately. I consider my self pretty much raised in the city. My dad moved into a house at 7th and Rodman Streets, while my mom got remarried and moved out to Malvern, Pennsylvania, when I was about five or six. My mom stayed married for about five or six years.

I attended K.D. Markley Public School in Malvern and saw my dad on weekends and on Sundays. I left K.D.M. after second grade and went into a private school in Westtown, Pennsylvania, where I am now. When I was about eight or so, my dad, still living in the city, got remarried. About a year or two later, they moved out of the city to Bala Cynwyd, Pennsylvania, where they live now. My mom got divorced (again!) when I was about ten or so. We moved to West Chester, Pennsylvania, which is *right* next to my current school, Westtown Friends School. Those are my current standings: I live with my mom in West Chester during the week. I see my dad in Bala Cynwyd on weekends and Wednesday nights. I'm a ninth grader at Westtown School.

So, as you can see, I've lived all over the place, but I consider my roots to be in Philly. My mom and I agree that living in suburbia (aka West Chester) really sucks compared to the city. The only reason we live out here is for my school. Once I graduate, my mom will probably move back into the city or into a more densely populated area. I know that I will definitely need to go to a college where there are a lot of people, close to a city. My dad and I usually spend part of our weekends together in the city. So, despite my dad's, my mom's, and my being transplanted to the 'burbs of Philadelphia, our hearts still lie in the city.

I don't have any brothers or sisters. I have a dog, Deke, that my mom and I got in November 1994. Despite their divorce, my parents are very good friends and have a great relationship together. I am very close to both sides of my extended family.

Mary Toth

I'm eighteen; my birth date is May 14th. My hometown is sort of an odd story because I spent the first five years of my life in Los Angeles, and I don't remember terribly much—you don't usually remember much between the ages of one and five. And then my parents got a bunch of money—actually, my dad won a bunch of money on *Jeopardy*—and we moved up to Willits, where we built our own house. He worked as a—I think he worked for a Northern California research institute for a while—and he was commuting from Willits because they like the rural aspects of it something or other. It wasn't LA. So, I grew up a lot in Willits—a really tiny town in Northern California, with I think, a thousand people. I think we knew when we hit a thousand people because we got our official McDonald's.

Half of the life that I had spent there was McDonald's-free, which was nice. I lived there for eight years—from five to about thirteen. I lived up on a mountain fifteen minutes away from the main drag, which was hardly extensive; I was kind of isolated—I'm an only child. So I lived up on a mountain with my two intellectual parents, and we lived about two blocks away from my mother's father and her aunt. That was our little family. We were fairly reclusive. My parents were always kind of reclusive, being LA-ites and everything, and so I had an odd socialization. I was actually much more comfortable with adults.

I spent those years in Willits as an outsider; nobody really got along with me, and I didn't really get along with anybody else. When I got to my teenage years, my parents decided that they didn't really want me to go to Willits High School, which, knowing Willits High School, I was kind of happy anyway. We moved to Healdsburg, California, so that the commute for my dad wouldn't be as hard, and we got a house up there. It was the middle of my sixth-grade year, so I spent junior high and high school in Healdsburg, which I consider more my hometown.

Healdsburg is where I came out. It's a small or middle-size town just north of Santa Rosa. It's bigger than Willits—4 or 5,000, somewhere in there. But, it's sort of rural; it has all the feel of a rural town. There are a lot of, oh, what you would classically refer to as hicks and rural folks, and there's a lot of culture conflict going on with the more touristy part of town—the upper- upper-class folks—the wine country sort of thing. And a lot of clash goes down between the folks who've been there all their lives who own vineyards or do the logging industry thing. There's a lot of culture conflict going on there that I had to deal with because the more rural folks are somewhat homophobic and that was a difficulty.

My home life was very odd—unpredictable—and that was very hard for me. And at the time, I mean, here I am an adolescent ball of angst anyway, so I'm going to take everything my family does personally. I hated that. All I would see is my mom being on a rampage. We had a lot of mother-daughter struggles over things like laundry, oddly enough—things that I thought wouldn't be such a big deal in normal families. It wasn't a terribly wonderful situation to come home to. Between that and not feeling accepted anywhere else, I mean, not accepted at school, not particularly happy at home, I also had a lot of grade pressure. Both my parents would put a lot of pressure on me; they were both intellectual, and my dad was a chemistry professor. I had an ulcer by the time I was fifteen. I also became somewhat alcoholic. My parents drink a lot, and I would like to classify that as alcoholic, although they wouldn't. But it was hard. At that point, practically on a weekly basis, if not a nightly basis, I would have to go down and tell my parents to turn the music down because I'm trying to get to sleep to go to school the next day. They'd be having a party and telling me that I'm being a party pooper and all this sort of thing, and I had to be the only responsible child in the household. So I sort of turned to that and said, "Okay, well, shit, I'll join in the party if it will get me to sleep any faster." And so I started drinking scotch fairly heavily; I think that contributed to the ulcer.

Paige

I'm eighteen, and my hometown is about sixty miles south of San Francisco. I've lived there ever since I was born. It's very suburban, upper class, about 30,000 people. It's been described as the breeding ground or a Disneyland for yuppies. I went to a small high school of 1,200 people. I have one sister who's twenty-five and a brother who is twenty. We all live together; my mom and dad, they're not divorced; they've been married for thirty-one years—disgustingly happy. My sister went to Berkeley, and she's going to medical school now. And my brother went to Chico, California, for two years and is now just hanging out. So we're a pretty normal family.

My dad's family has some serious, serious, serious family troubles. In November of last year, when I went to school, I started having some really bad nightmares. I went and saw a therapist and asked her about these nightmares, and we started doing some kind of hypnosis-type exercises. What I've come to realize is that when I was nine and ten, and once when I was eleven, my uncle had raped me. This is something I just realized I'd blocked totally out of my mind. There's nothing I can do about it now, obviously. But I knocked on my aunt's door and told her, and she slammed the door in my face and told me to get lost. My mother's been really supportive. My mother said, "You can either try to solve this and let it consume your life, or take it in stride and deal with it; you have some of the best counseling available to you and can prevent it from happening again in our family." So that's the road I've chosen. I'd like to say that I could blame all my troubles since I was eleven on it, but I can't. I just have to go on.

Todd Fay-Long

I'm seventeen; I'll turn eighteen in December. I live with my mom and her husband and my twelve-year-old brother; I'm out to all of them, and it's good. I live in Petaluma, California, which is about an hour north of San Francisco; I don't know how many people live there. It's pretty much suburbia. It's like a small town mentality anyway. There's a downtown area that a lot of people hang out in. Some of my friends hang out there. I've hung out downtown since I was fourteen so I know pretty much everybody who hangs out around downtown. I live in a brand new tract housing development. It depresses me because it used to be a field. When I first moved to Petaluma, there were fields all around my house, and now it's houses everywhere. I'm hopefully going to move to San Francisco in June to go to school there. I'm planning on going to Harvey Milk Institute. It's a gay and lesbian studies school.

I was born in Minneapolis, Minnesota. We lived there for about a year, and then we moved to Columbus, Ohio. We lived there for about two years. We moved to Pacifica, California, and lived there until I was in third grade. It wasn't until we moved to Petaluma—I guess I was in fifth grade—that people started calling me a "faggot," that kinda stuff. I didn't have very many friends in elementary school. I was mostly just friends with all the rejects and dorks.

I started fighting with my mom a lot then, and my mom was with this guy I didn't get along with, so that was kind of hard. He wasn't a homophobic person, I don't think. We just didn't get along. Our personalities just clashed. So I was grounded all the time. One night I stayed out all night; my mom was supposed to come pick me up and I just wasn't there and I didn't call or anything. I went to work the next day and my mom showed up; we got in this huge fight and went home, screaming at each other. I said something like, "Well, if you don't want me to live here, then I'll just find another place to live." I meant I'll go stay at a friend's house and let us cool down, but she interpreted that to mean, "Okay, I'm sending you to live with your dad."

So I moved to my dad's in Rohnert Park, which is right above Petaluma, but it's even worse than Petaluma because there's not even a downtown; it's total suburbia. It's all shopping centers and houses. So, I went to a high school there called Rancho Cotati. I didn't know anybody, so I wasn't the center of attention and people weren't calling me "fag" and stuff like that. But, living with my dad was really hard because my dad was raised to think that being gay is wrong, and he very much believed that. So I wasn't out to anybody then.

Jim

I'm seventeen and my birth date is September 27th. I live in Pleasanton, California. The bubble, that is. It's a little piece-of-shit town. It's pretty small; there's only 10,000 people there, I think. I have lived in Pleasanton all my life. I have one sister, Jamie, and my mom and dad.

Chapter 2

One of These Kids Is Not Like the Others

COMING OUT: THE ONGOING SAGA

So much of knowing someone (knowing oneself) involves simple acts of information exchange. Describing living situations, dates, friendships, experiences in class or at work generates a great deal of anxiety for those trying to hide the queer pieces of their lives. To truly share oneself with others, a certain amount of honesty must exist, and many people find it unbearable to constantly lie to themselves or others about their queerness.

The phrase "coming out" has so many unspoken, yet understood, meanings to those in or connected to the queer community. Coming out refers not to a single moment or event but rather an ongoing revelation and performance of self that comes into play each time someone new, or perhaps familiar, (re)enters a queer person's life.

The narratives in Chapters 2, 3, and 4 discuss what it means to come out to oneself, family, and community. There is no lineality or progression intended by the order of the chapters. Acting on one's desires may happen long before there is a connection or declaration made regarding sexual identity. Perhaps that is what makes the process of coming out so dynamic and unique within the context of queer history spanning the past four decades.

For many older gay, lesbian, and bi people, coming out was not an option. Although queer communities existed, they were often only visible in larger urban areas and rarely involved straight friends or family members. A clear line of demarkation was made between one's straight world and one's queer world. If you had found other queers, there was no identity to declare per se, only desires to explore and pursue. It was somewhat unthinkable to discuss these desires with one's parents and friends, as desire for the same gender was still widely considered a mental illness until the early 1970s and, arguably, well past that decade. The social stigma and lack of information surrounding queer sexualities left few options for the expression of sexual identities other than the heterosexual norm.

The boundaries between straight and queer worlds have eroded slowly over the past four decades. Increased public dialogue regarding sexual identity has led to the meshing of once very separate realities. Young people now have an opportunity to not only question but reject the heterosexual norm, determining the expression of their sexuality and often engaging their parents, friends, and society at large in this process.

Although the process of coming out is ongoing for many of the speakers in this collection, each describes an identifiable, albeit fuzzy, starting point. Several young people recount the pivotal moment they acknowledged an attraction to someone of the same gender or to both genders, to themselves. This self-realization, for many, may lead to posing the reflective question, "Are these just passing feelings or how I have always felt?"

For some, these reflections recall clarifying, affirming memories of attractions to others of the same gender at early ages; for others, no confirming childhood memories exist. Regardless of the outcome of such soul-searching, the desire for, and compelling attraction to, members of the same or both genders persists.

Whether one recalls feeling such attractions at an early age or later in life, a highly political, symbolic action takes place when a link is made between these feelings and one's identity; when someone moves from unspoken desires to action and seeks out a supportive community to validate those desires and actions, coming out is transformed from a singular act to a cultural statement with significance beyond the individual.

Ironically, such bold statements of identity are received with some skepticism by a resistant and suspicious adult world. Teachers, parents, and even adults in the queer community often have a difficult time accepting that a fourteen-year-old could "know" his or her sexuality identity. As these narratives attest, many adults miss the point. Young people are just as capable of exploring or asserting their sexual identity as adults.

Coming out, as expressed by the narratives in these chapters, encompasses facing the challenges of accepting desires yet to be fully validated by mainstream society while risking the rejection (or worse) of friends and family. The personal, in this case, is most definitely political. The costs are potentially high, but as you will read, the rewards can be freedom from oppressive silence and an opportunity to truly embrace and love oneself.

* * *

Anthony Gomez

I started to come out to myself when I was probably . . . oh, I'd have to say around eight. I remember once, I saw this guy and I thought about him in my mind. This was when I was seven. I just love the look of a man's body. Blonds are my weakness for some reason. Blonds and surfers are my weakness. There was this guy at school, and he was so fine; I said, "Oh, God, he is so cute!" And one of my friends heard me say this and asked me, "Are you gay?" I actually didn't know what to say.

If this was a phase, I would know, okay? It's not a phase. I like guys. And I don't believe it's a phase. I think that I'm full-blown gay. I do my hip thing; I swish, and I know what I like. And it's like, "Who is anyone to tell me what I'm going through, okay?" They're not up in my head.

Then I started hearing a lot more about people being gay and it really opened my eyes. I thought, "That's what I am." I found out more about the gay community by just talking to people. I found out what all the emblems meant; I went to groups, I went to coffee shops to meet people. I was reading newspapers and books.

My friends call me either a flame, the little queen, or the little princess. But if somebody calls me that and they use it in a derogatory way, I get very defensive. I will tend to fight back. So I usually don't mind those words, unless they're meant to hurt me.

Sometimes I think, "Goddamn, I hate my life; it's not going anywhere." But then other days I feel so uplifted, as if dealing with being gay is gonna make me stronger in a way.

Adam Hardy

I remember having a fascination with other boys as early as third grade. They just seemed more *interesting* than the girls, even though I didn't identify it as an attraction as such. I didn't have very many friends in elementary school. The few I did have were mostly girls (with one exception), and they were all really bright.

However, around fourth or fifth grade, I got a burst of self-esteem when I was invited into the program for gifted students. It was the first time I didn't consider myself to be dumb (which was what the other kids called me). As a sidenote, I've always been terribly body shy, and I have vivid memories of being *terrified* whenever my friends asked me to spend the night at their houses, though I don't know if my reasons involved my sexuality back then. I know they ended up that way.

I found myself in an extraordinarily accepting school environment around sixth or seventh grade, which was good because I needed that extra support when I began to notice that I was "different" from everyone else. Like most people, I think I knew I was gay since I first began having romantic feelings toward others, but I denied that fact to myself for a long time.

I can actually remember the process of lying in bed at night and agonizing, thinking "I can't possibly be *that* way." Homosexuality had a lot of connotations back then, which I picked up almost entirely from other kids at school. Among adults, it was simply never discussed. But the kids talked about it, in xenophobic tones of "them" and "they," making gays out to be something between vampires and comic foils, always conveniently either demeaned or demonized. I went through a stage in coming out to myself where I said, "All right, I'm homosexual, but I'm not one of *them,*" because of course I was attracted to men, but I wasn't . . . (insert all the nasty things that gays were supposed to be).

It's difficult for me to talk about the process of coming out to myself, really, in concrete terms because I've repressed so much of it. It has come back in bits and pieces, as I've read others' experiences and had sudden moments of realization that "Oh my God! I went through that too!"

Ivan Velez Jr. has written a couple of comic series dealing with issues of homosexuality. *Tales from the Closet* is supposed to be very good, and I've heard of some gay support groups who've gotten hold of it. Velez also writes *Blood Syndicate,* published by DC's Milestone imprint, which features one of the only realistically written comic book heroes around: Fade. I mention this because in a few panels in one of the issues Fade is wrestling with his homosexuality, which a mind-reading villain pointed out to him. He says something to the effect of, "I couldn't stand my friends looking at me and *knowing* . . ." This was precisely what I felt.

I was convinced by the actions of the kids around me at school that if any of my friends knew, they'd never be comfortable around me again, and that terrified me more than anything else. I've since developed a theory that public schooling is one of the most painful and detrimental things we can put kids through, particularly gay teenagers. If I hadn't been going to school on a daily basis, I doubt I would have come as close as I did to committing suicide.

I think I finally came to terms with my homosexuality somewhere around seventh grade (I was twelve?), when I fell in love with my best friend Lewis. Lewis was intelligent, very attractive . . . hell, he was my best friend. Didn't help that I had to change with him in the locker room every day—another invention of straight men to torture gay high-schoolers. I found myself thinking about him at night, and actively denying to myself that I was doing so. The human mind is capable of some amazing feats. Eventually, one night, I remember saying to myself, "All right. We're going to have to say the 'H' word." I couldn't manage "gay." "Gay" was going too far. "Gay" was one step away from "fag."

Alan Wiley

I was a total queen in elementary school. I took gymnastics for four years; I loved hopscotch. I hated football and soccer and baseball, but I did play some sports. I just collected Chinese jacks, played on the bars, and I did all the typical girlie things.

I flamed a lot; I had the total limp wrist in elementary school. But through the course of elementary school, I learned that that just wasn't okay. You know, "Guys could not go to gymnastics"; "Guys could not play hopscotch." So I stopped doing that, and I started trying to butch myself up and get not really masculine but just to the point where I wasn't being called names. And I was successful with that.

Once I got to junior high, it just didn't come naturally to me to act feminine anymore. It was more instinctive for me to act masculine, and I still act masculine pretty much now. It's weird because before I came out, I felt like I really had to act masculine because otherwise I'd be called a fag. And once I came out, I was already being called a fag so it didn't matter. I feel like I act the most natural now than I ever have before.

I first realized I was gay when I was around four years old. I knew I was attracted to men, and I didn't know what to call it, and I didn't think there was anything different about it. I just thought it was normal. And then as I got into junior high, I realized that that wasn't normal, and that I was different somehow, and I became really aware that I was different. But, I still denied that I was gay, and I was a big homophobe, and I called everyone a faggot, and I was a total jerk.

I remember writing a journal my freshman/sophomore year in high school, and I was so afraid of being gay, but I still needed to deal with it. So in my journal, I never mentioned being gay. I called it Problem No. 1. I would write things like, "Well, I have this problem and I have that problem, but none of that really matters because I have Problem No. 1, and so my life is just gonna suck anyway and I might as well die." It's weird how I was dealing with it; I was so afraid of it that I wouldn't even mention it. I had to give it another name. And last year, I just looked back on this journal and I read it; it was such an uplifting experience for me because I saw how depressed I was then and how near death I was then and how I am now.

Now I'm nineteen and I identify as being gay. I have identified as being gay for around three years now, since about my sophomore year in high school. I was out to close friends as being gay. I came out in high school to my writing seminar class; that's the first time I came out to everybody. And what I had was a surprise for my class; I could have the whole class period for myself and just do whatever I wanted to. I talked to my teacher, and I decided that I wanted to come out to the class, and he thought it was great. So, I brought in my best friend, who lived with me at the time, who's a straight guy I was also totally in love with—that's a different story. I brought him in so the kids could understand from a straight perspective what it was like to know a gay person. And I just told them all that I was gay, and I answered questions for an hour and a half; that's how I came out in high school. And fifteen minutes after the class was over, everyone knew, and that's when the harassment started at school.

When I was younger, the only reason I didn't flame out was because I was afraid of being called a fag. And now I'm not afraid of being called a fag anymore, so what do I care. I should just act the way I want to act.

When I was first coming out in high school—actually, right before I came out in high school—I was talking to one of my counselors in charge of the peer counseling program at my school. I talked to her about coming out and she told me she thought I was a really courageous person for doing this. I told her that I didn't feel like I was courageous at all; I felt really scared, like a total wuss. She told me something that made me feel good about myself: courage isn't about doing something when you're confident about doing it; courage is about doing something when you're scared out of your mind. That was the first time in my life I really felt like I actually was being courageous and I was doing something good. I don't even know why I came out. I really didn't need to. But I just knew what I was going through, I guess, and I didn't want anyone else to have to go through that in the same way.

I'd been told so often that being gay was disgusting that I kinda believed it after a while. I'd been told so often, "Those fucking fags, that is so gross . . . queers getting it on with each other . . . it's just really disgusting." I never thought it was disgusting, but it really took a lot to get over that. I went from being really homophobic to being open to gay ideas, and then I came out. But in high school, once I came out, I was wearing freedom rings to school every day. When I would play concerts with my tuba and my tuxedo, I'd have my freedom rings outside my tuxedo. I wanted to be really visible. I just wish people would know that I was gay right away. That's why I have to wear freedom rings and stuff like that, 'cause I feel if I don't, then people are gonna think I'm straight, and I don't want them to think that.

I have a lot of friends in SF who don't have a set sexuality. When I first came up to San Francisco, I wasn't hanging out with gay people really. Now I'm just meeting more and more people, and they just happen to be sexually ambiguous, and we get along great. I really like the queer friends I've made up here. I figured I would have more queer friends coming up to San Francisco.

I just want to say something specifically about homophobia and my own internalized homophobia. I was extremely afraid of being called gay. I knew I was, and I felt if someone called me gay, they'd figured me out somehow and that that was gonna be the end of my life. I was petrified of being called gay. And once I realized that that was just a dumb fear, and once I'd accepted myself and was coming out, I realized that I was getting called gay and fag anyway. I could have taken it in an offensive way, "How dare he call me a fag." But, it got to the point where they would call me a fag, and I would say, "You are right, that's exactly what I am, I'm a big, old fag. Yeah! Okay, let's just put it on a big poster now . . . I don't care . . . you can do whatever." I took that fear of being exposed, that fear of being called "gay," away from myself.

I readily identify as a queer; I've taken the fear out of those words. I'm not afraid of them anymore. You have a choice in any situation such as this. You can either let yourself get down on yourself and get really scared and freak out, or you can just accept it for what it is and incorporate it into your life. And that's what I've done with the word queer. I'm not afraid of being a freak. Walking around in Mormonland with long purple hair is gonna make you a freak anyway, and I'd become accustomed to it. I'm not afraid to stand out; I'm not afraid to voice my opinion, even if it's different from anyone else's. I embrace the word queer, and I think it's great. I don't personally understand why people don't like the word queer. It encompasses the whole gay/lesbian/bisexual/transgender community, it's short, and it's one syllable. It's a great word all around.

I took the weapons away from all the homophobes around me. The only thing that they could get me with was calling me gay. If I'm totally out being gay and don't care what I get called because of it, then they can't hurt me anymore. I think that's probably the best part about being out. I get called a fag all the time, and it doesn't affect me, because I am a fag. So, it's the truth, and I've accepted the truth, and I'm not afraid of it anymore.

Eileene Coscolluela

I came out to myself the end of my junior year in high school, so I have been out to myself for the past three years. I came out to myself when I began to meet other gays, lesbians, and bisexuals, and they were just wonderful people. Just knowing them made me start questioning my sexuality. Then June came around, June 1992, and since that is lesbian and gay pride month, I just became aware of gayness and saw all the TV shows on the local public television station, and I just learned more about it.

I then started questioning my sexuality, and I came out as being bisexual. I look back, and I realize that I've always had an attraction to members of the same sex and that I've had fantasies about it. Come to think of it, I never denied it to myself; I just never outwardly thought about it. If anything, I'm a heterosexually inclined bisexual. But I hate labels. I just consider myself completely queer and proud.

Dawn McCausland

I was about fourteen or fifteen when I started to get really close to my female friends. Just very close, very affectionate; I wanted to spend all my time with them. I started getting obsessed in a sense. I got jealous of their boyfriends; I wanted my female friends all to myself; I wanted to be around them all the time; I wanted to cuddle with them; I wanted to sleep in their beds. Small hints like that. But, it was an interesting time because I was dating guys the entire time and had some pretty intimate relationships with guys. I had boyfriends.

What was the most fascinating thing about that though is, I was basically best friends with most of my boyfriends, and I arranged it, unconsciously in a way, that I got involved with boys all living about 3,000 miles away.

In that way, I got the affection, someone who cared about me, I got a best friend, and all the communication. A lot of my boyfriends had a very strong feminine side. In that way, I never had to deal with the sex and I never had to deal with confronting how much I didn't really want to be around guys. When I was ten or eleven, I did a lot of boy things and I was very active. But then later on, I was always more mature for my age, very self-conscious, and so I did girl things that didn't require very much physical activity, didn't require so much competition.

So I hung out with girls a lot. When I first started dealing with my lesbian feelings, I had a very close friend whom I had a crush on; It was my sophomore year. I didn't really realize it until I got very obsessive about her. I wanted to be the most important thing in her life; I wanted her to just totally depend on me, open up to me, and let me be the only thing in her life. And I would go over to her house and I'd be falling asleep on her bed and feel this sense of almost being cheated that I didn't get to sleep with her or kiss her, and I started to realize it. When I first started dealing with it, it was very, very hard, and I wouldn't admit to it at all. I would try to write about it in my journal, and I would not be able to spell out her name. I used initials or code names. And it wasn't really that I was afraid that other people would find it. It was that I couldn't witness myself writing it. I couldn't see it; I couldn't admit it. And so, it was either that I had to do a code name and explain it, or I had to use her name and not explain it. So that was kind of hard.

Then I started to deal with these feelings; I thought that there was no way that I could possibly be gay because I didn't fit the stereotype and because I was the girl that grew up in the dresses, and, to an extent, I liked that. I liked playing with dolls. In a lot of ways, I was a very feminine person and fit in a lot of female stereotypical roles. Not necessarily that I wanted to settle down and get a family or anything, but I just enjoyed girl things.

Even though I grew up in a very liberal household that was accepting of gay people, I collected everything that the culture taught me about gay people, and I kept it in a file in the back of my brain, and I didn't realize it was there. Issues of gay rights were discussed fairly often in my family; it would seem that my coming-out process would be very easy because my parents had been supportive. But, growing up, it was always discussed as a political issue, and it was never a personal issue. There was never any possibility that either myself or anyone else in my family would turn out being gay. Which is actually quite funny, because by stereotypic analysis, my sister should be a dyke. She was on the boy's junior high football team and looked like a boy, dressed like a boy, did all the boy things.

But what's funny about that is I found out later, when I thought about it, everyone in my family was given very specific roles. Even though there was a fair amount of acceptance of my sister's oddness, you might say, it was still very defined. I was the one who was always wearing the dresses, played with Barbies, had my tea set. So it was expected that I would keep up that role. I think it was especially expected that I would be straight and stay in traditionally defined feminine roles.

When it had to do with other people, I always said, "Oh, well, I don't have a problem with gay people," and "I'm not homophobic." I even had bumper stickers about it and this whole thing. But, when it came to me, it was a whole other issue, and I realized that I had stocked up all of this prejudice and all of these stereotypes. When suddenly all those things that the culture had told me actually applied to me, I just felt like nobody would accept me, and I got really depressed, in this kind of black hole about it. It was a horrible time.

When you grow up with the culture's ideas of what I was, messages like "gay people are sick," "gay people are wrong," "they're dysfunctional," or "they had a bad childhood"—all of these just fucked up things—when I tried to fit in all those boxes, it didn't make sense. When you hear it as "those people are that way," and then suddenly you are one of those people, it becomes "you're that way." So "I'm sick," "I'm wrong," "I'm not okay." It was a challenge to deal with. But, I realized that it was the culture telling me that, and that society and the people who aren't gay don't know me.

I remember asking myself a very basic question: "Well, who knows me better, them or me? Do I know what my intentions are? Am I having sick, immoral, wrong thoughts? Or is that someone else's judgment on somebody they don't know?" So I realized, no, I had this real honest connection and crush on someone. That's natural. And it's not sick.

I always thought that there was, in some way, a formula for being gay. If you looked like this and you acted like this and you had this kind of relationship and you didn't like guys and all these really stereotypic things, then you were gay. You would just know it right off the bat. I had some interesting relationships with some of my best friends, but other than that, I didn't feel like I knew right away, and so I had to go through this whole process of questioning and comparing myself to other people and psychoanalyzing everything. Processing, processing, processing. I'd like people to know that it's just not that simple. Sure, after a point, you will get to where you just know. But it's not necessarily right off the bat.

Especially after my first girlfriend, I went into denial for a while. Then, after I went through my whole equations on how much do I like guys compared to how much I like girls, then I realized that I just knew. That's just where I wanted to be. I started writing almost fantasy papers about my feelings for women. I realized I had never done that before. I went back through letters from old boyfriends after I had broken up with my first girlfriend. I realized that I really didn't sit around and think about them that much or really fantasize about us. When I was reading these letters from them, I realized they sounded like letters that I had written in my journals to my first girlfriend. I could imagine writing for her or for another girl the way they wrote for me, but I could never write for a guy that way. So I just knew.

It was really hard because I felt like people wouldn't believe me, especially since I came out as bi. "Oh, you just want to be trendy." But then I met lots of gay people, did a lot of coming out, did a lot of talking, went through a lot of my own internalized homophobia.

I remember the gay youth support group the first day I went very vividly because not only was I seeing my first gay people and having my first gay interactions, but I was defining myself that way, which was probably the scariest part. I just remember that first day because, when I was asked to talk, I was so freaked out. It was like crossing that line where I don't remember anything. I don't remember what I said; I don't remember who was there, what they looked like, what their expressions were. It was just this big white light. I was totally on the spot and my heart was pounding. I mean, I'm a fairly confident person. But, I was so freaked out. It was probably one of the scariest experiences of my life.

Eriq Chang

I identify as bisexual, and have since I was about six or seven. It was pretty firm; I pretty much knew. I came out to myself when I was ten. I really didn't understand the whole thing. I sort of experimented when I was young. I pretty much knew that it wasn't normal.

At that time, I knew I wasn't supposed to like guys, that I was supposed to like girls, but I wasn't attracted totally to one sex. I guess I just found that I liked both. At that age, I was pretty comfortable with myself. I came out as bi two years ago, and in Pleasanton, that's fairly difficult. But it was eventual. It was a process that I did.

I really feel like I'm on my own now, and I'm open about who I am. Because, for me, if you're not comfortable with your own sexuality, then you're not going to comfortable with someone else's.

I can never just hang out with straight guys. I've actually been able to hang out with a lot of straight guys, but I couldn't talk about sex and things that are less superficial. I have a lot of straight friends, and I have a lot of bi and gay/lesbian friends. But with straight guys, we're either looking at other women or else we're talking about sports or something. I don't feel like I can talk about my whole self. Ninety percent of my friends are girls.

Ernie Hsiung

I knew I was gay at an early age—of course, I didn't know it was being "gay," but I felt a close desire to be with guys my age as early as age five. I knew the feelings I felt had a name by junior high. It was also about this time when I knew it was "bad." My parents are Chinese immigrants, very conservative, and Christian. Bad things, when you're growing up and coming to realize you're gay. I wanted to be the good son, so I've always done what I was told. Unfortunately, that also meant a lot of pain, not being true to my own feelings.

Kyallee Santanders

Flip a coin. Heads or tails. Male or female. Black or white. Gay or straight. Absolutes. What happens if the coin lands on its side? What happens if the coin falls down the drain? I was born an "it." I climbed trees and played with the boys as well as played dress up with my female friends. I didn't want to be a boy or a girl; I was happy being an "it." I knew I was somehow different from the other kids, but there wasn't a name for it. Even the other kids sensed that I was different; I was called "queer" at nine years old by some older kids, and I had no idea what it meant.

I didn't think much about my lack of sexuality. I just wasn't interested in dating while growing up. I couldn't understand what all the fuss was about. All of my friends were raving about how cute this or that guy was, and I just didn't get it. They were boys. They had always been boys, and they'd always be boys in my eyes.

I didn't have a name for what I was until my sophomore year in high school. I was talking with a teacher, Lena, about sexual abuse, and I asked if she'd discussed it with her significant other. After a while, I noticed that she always answered my queries with "we" and not "he." I finally asked her if I was making an assumption. She said I was.

Doors opened. Suddenly, it was possible to be lesbian. I had met a real live lesbian who was well adjusted and in a long-term relationship. Still, the idea of being lesbian was scary, so it was quite awhile before I came out, even to myself.

The Amendment 2 campaign—an effort to remove sexual orientation from nondiscrimination clauses—pushed me even farther into the closet. I couldn't believe that Colorado voters could so openly discriminate against a group of people based on whom they loved. I did not want to acknowledge that I was part of this discriminated-against group. I called my teacher, Lena, the morning after the election and cried for an hour over the phone. What was this world coming to?

I fought my way out of the closet a mere three months later. A social worker got involved and told me to try to keep it to myself until college. She even called Lena in to help convince me. "I can't," I cried. "This is happening now, this is happening to me, and it's very real to me." Reluctantly, the social worker located a support group for gay teens—El Paso County support group. That was the beginning of my path out of the closet.

I identify as lesbian. Since coming out, I've talked with my oldest brother—he's seventeen—and he's dealing okay. I'm sure my mother has told a few relatives so they could cry together, but since coming out, we don't talk about it. And I guess that's okay for now, but someday she's going to have to start dealing with me as who I am, not who she thinks I am. Right now I guess I'm just letting her get used to the idea that I'm not who she thinks I am. I hate the secrecy, though, and the feeling of tiptoeing on ice around everyone, especially my younger siblings.

Lisa Campbell

When I was in eighth grade, I was having these dreams about women. And I'm thinking, "Wait, wait, wait, something's wrong here." I didn't say anything to anybody about that because I knew what goes on back there in Louisiana. In fact, one of my mom's friends asked me if I was gay, right in front of my mom. I was thirteen. She just asked me. And I was, like, "No! . . . Absolutely not!" They had been talking about a friend of theirs whose son was gay, and he was a few years older than me. It was not a good situation for him. I didn't really know him that well. I'd hung out with him a few times when I was younger. There were a lot of rumors going around about him, and he was pretty much persecuted. When my mom and her friend were talking, they were like, "Oh, his poor father." But what about the poor kid, you know?

My freshman year, I started to realize a lot of things, and that's when I started to label myself a lesbian. Before then, I didn't really call it anything; I didn't have a name, or I didn't put a name on it.

The biggest thing that helped me out was watching tennis. I like tennis. They did an interview with one of my favorite players, Martina Navratilova. Well, in Louisiana, I'd watched some tennis, but I never knew that she was gay. Then I moved out here and I was sitting watching TV. Something was said about her being a lesbian. My dad was watching the TV too, and I said, "Dad, isn't that, um . . . ?" He said, "Yes." I answered, "Oh, okay."

It seemed okay for Martina Navratilova; she was out to the whole world. I spent the whole summer thinking. I was painting my dad's deck; I had hours and hours just to think. It was the summer before high school. I'm thinking all the time, "Wait, how can she be a lesbian?" What about her family and all that stuff? I read, the next year, the autobiography that she'd written. It helped me out a little bit.

I stayed in the closet for a couple years after that summer. After I started driving in my sophomore year, I had access to go get books that I wanted to read. I used to hide books from my parents. I was reading *Venus Envy* by Rita Mae Brown. If I could hear them coming up the stairs, I'd hide the book!

Eventually, in my junior year, I started coming out. I asked a friend of mine for help 'cause I knew her mom was a psychologist;

I knew she'd probably be able to help me out. I asked her, "Who would you talk to if you had no one to talk to?" She named off all these people, all this list. And I said, "No, no; I can't talk to the family; no, not friends; no."

She knew I was really frustrated about life in general. I was very down and depressed, and she knew that I was probably slipping back into a phase where I would be suicidal again. She didn't want to see me there, and I didn't want to see me there. She said, "Well, you know, my mom can probably refer you to somebody. Or would you want to talk to my mom?" I said, "No, I want to talk to somebody I don't know, who has nothing to do with my life." Her mom, the psychologist, referred me to a friend of hers.

When I went into the session, it was funny, 'cause I was nervous. I'm just sitting in there in the chair in the waiting room thinking, "I have to tell her. . . . How am I going to tell her? . . . I came here to tell her. . . . I'm paying to tell her."

We finally walk in the room; I'm sitting in the chair, my hands were sweating. I talked about other things going on in my life. At the time I started therapy, only my grandmother had been diagnosed with cancer. A few weeks later my grandfather was diagnosed as well. He ended up dying from it. My grandmother is actually almost in remission now. So I'm sitting there, telling her all this, and then I go, "Um, um, by the way, I'm gay." I didn't look at her; I was looking at the corner of the room, and I just kept talking. I tried to slide it in there. I had this huge argument going on in my head before I said anything. This one side of me is saying, "No, don't tell her, don't tell her, don't tell her," then this other side is saying, "You're going to tell her, you paid to tell her. She has nothing to do with your life. You're going to tell her!" Finally, after just arguing in my head, I told her, and it was like, "Oh, thank God!, I told someone."

She didn't have any response at all. It didn't faze her, and I figured, she's either really good at this, or she's gay.

She ended up giving me a copy of the *Bay Times* at the end of the session. By the next session, I knew for sure she was gay because she said she had done some work at the Pacific Center—a gay support center. I was very comfortable after I found out that she was gay. It was like, "Okay, now it's not such a big deal."

The psychologist I was going to persuaded me to go to the youth group at Pacific Center, and so I went. The first time I went, I was doing all this behind my parents' backs. My parents knew none of this. They thought I was going to the movies quite a bit with Shalyn and Renee. Those are the two friends I had covering for me all the time. Or they thought I'd gone out shopping. At Christmastime, I could get by with that excuse. I would go, and I'd get out of school early. I'd go and shop fifteen minutes. My stepmom's the type of person who takes hours to pick out stuff, and so she'd figure I'd probably spend a couple hours out shopping.

I had kept what I was really doing all to myself. I kept it in. It was really tough. I would go through the day, and I would think about it almost every minute of the day thinking, "I can't do this anymore." There were several times in that August, before my grandmother was diagnosed with cancer, that I had called my grandfather with the purpose of telling him, because I knew he was the one person who loved me very unconditionally, and he would not care. Or he'd be able to help me in some way. I was just looking for somebody to say either "You're going to Hell" or "You're okay." I was just on that line. Whichever one I ran into first, I would have accepted.

Mathis

Well, the first time I knew I was gay was when I was three. I was molested by two girl cousins—I'm not gay because of that by the way. I remember thinking, even when it was happening, that this shouldn't be happening because I like boys. And that was my first memory of sexual identity at all. Then after that, it was in the back of my head; I always thought about it.

I messed around with some friends I had and stuff, and then, when I was ten, I started talking to my mother's boyfriend—and I started telling him, that I had feelings toward boys and stuff like that. At the time, I had this friend who was absolutely gorgeous, and I had a total crush on him, and I told my mother's boyfriend about it. It ended up that he used that to start a sexual relationship with me, and it lasted till I was seventeen.

And then, after what started happening at home, I started losing control of my home life. I didn't have anything that felt stable; I was living a total lie. I was lying to my mother; I was lying to my friends; I was lying to everybody. I couldn't be home with my stepfather because he didn't want a relationship; he just wanted to use me for sex. I started feeling like I couldn't tell anybody. And for me, I think, coming out was part of dealing with what had happened with my stepfather. I never really dealt with what had happened when I was three with my cousins because I don't remember it; I don't know exactly what happened. I remember certain things. I still have images in my mind, and I know that those things happened, but I never really dealt with it.

I told my mom when I was thirteen that my stepfather was molesting me. My mother didn't do anything. She just told me that if my stepfather ever did it again for me to tell her. About two or three months later, it just started happening again. I never told her again until I was seventeen, which is actually when I officially came out to her. I figured that since she didn't do anything the first time, then she wouldn't do anything if I told her again. I don't have that good of a relationship with my mom now, which I guess is to be expected. She is still with this man, which I really disapprove of. But it's her life, and I can't control her life, only she can.

I don't consider what my stepfather did to me child molestation, even though it was really. I consider it to be rape because through that, my mother's boyfriend totally destroyed my relationship with my mother. That wasn't my first sexual experience, so I'm not scarred by it or anything. I'm just more upset at the emotional part of it. He was very manipulative, and he showed me a lot of attention. I really wasn't getting that from anybody at the time, because at school I was having a lot of problems. I'm slowly getting over it, and I know it will take a lot of time, but a lot of my coming out to myself is wrapped up in this stuff.

I am proud because I'm gay, because being gay is a part of who I am, and I am proud of myself. Some of my friends are very straight acting, and they have to wear T-shirts and stuff like that. We've had hour-long conversations about it. For me, it was never something I had to present to people. People could always tell I was gay the minute they saw me, which sometimes bothers me. I wish sometimes it weren't like that. My friends are always doing something to just totally out themselves the minute people see them. Well, for me, I don't need to do that. I've been told that I'm not femme, I'm not butch, I'm in the middle. So for me, if people want to assume something about me, they can assume it. But they're gonna have to talk to me to find out the truth.

Michael Talis

At this point, I'm still classifying myself. I am definitely gay and am more attracted to men than women. But, I am also attracted to women a lot and have had several girlfriends in the past. So, though I don't really like to admit it, I'm probably bisexual.

The reason why I don't like to admit it is because I either want to be *gay* or *straight,* no in-betweens. But it seems that I am in between—bisexual—and there's nothing I can do about it.

Mary Toth

At a young age, I'd basically determined that I would have rather have been a boy, simply because I didn't know how to interact with girls. My mom never taught me that traditional female roles were something to pursue. She was very much a feminist, started the NOW chapter for Pasadena and things like that. So I knew that the accepted norms were not right, but I had no basis to go from—my mom was a punk, but I didn't really want to embrace that. But also, I didn't know what else to go to.

I tried to become feminine and just failed miserably. It was sad. I did have a boyfriend in my freshman year of high school, and I did wear dresses all the time because I thought that's what he wanted, and I was being a good little submissive girl. At that point, this was the first guy who ever asked me out. He was the first person who ever asked me. I don't think it mattered that he was a guy. I was looking for anything as a source of stability. So I wore dresses that I thought he would like, and my mom sort of encouraged this, and I didn't really know how to take it. My mom was at a loss with me anyway. Here's this angry child who doesn't fit in anywhere. What are you going to encourage?

I'd constantly get at home that you should not do anything with the status quo, don't behave like the other kids, blah, blah, blah, blah, blah, and don't conform. And here I am thinking, "Okay, well, I'm not conforming, and I'm getting persecuted all the time. . . . what do I do?" So, I just turned into this ball of junior high angst and decided that it was easier for me to enculturate myself as a tomboy and sort of become invisible to that whole culture of femininity.

But I remember my first lesbian feeling was when I was about the age of . . . oh, heavens . . . I was in first grade or so. I was really young, and I fell madly in love with a girl in high school. She took the bus that I took, and I was always getting crushed out. I actually asked her out because I didn't know that girls weren't supposed to ask girls out, and I'd always considered myself somewhat more of a boy anyway. I was a wild child anyway. I wasn't classically feminine or anything like that, being a tomboy in the woods. Anyway, so I asked her out, and then my parents sort of said, "Okay, this is cute," but it was just implied that this wasn't really something to be taken seriously or anything like that.

There was something of a progression in my attractions to people. You see, I've always been somewhat of a highly sexual person. That was part of my motivation. I realized, Okay, now I can have sex with people whom I actually want to have sex with. And now I can go out and find them. If you traced all the boys I'd had crushes on, they were getting increasingly more effeminate. They had always been fairly effeminate. Then it got to the point where I was only having crushes on obviously gay men. Then I realized this is a step away from being crushed out on a woman. And then it all made sense: I'm a lesbian.

I was fourteen when I started realizing that I was a lesbian. It started appearing in my journals and through various interactions. All through junior high, I'd been desperately afraid of women, which was kind of funny. And I'd only hung out with boys mostly. I was the quintessential tomboy, and a lot of that was that I was afraid of associating myself with women. I think part of that was due to an underlying fear that if a woman gave me a hug or something, I'd enjoy it, and that totally freaked me out. So I had a lot of internalized homophobia that just kept me in this little ball of adolescent tension.

All the friends I'd had in junior high and high school, which were the friends whom I came out to first, were all tomboys too. They were all being socially rejected, and I figured that 99.9 percent of 'em were all dykes too. But there was one friend of mine who was traditionally feminine. And the only traditionally feminine role that I really partook of was playing classical flute in the band; that was where I developed a friendship with somebody who would be considered traditionally feminine in hippie-type fashion.

I had my first crush on my music teacher, and that made me admit that I was a lesbian. I was literally walking up to my mirror every day for about, oh, a month and a half, looking in the mirror every day after school and saying, "I am not a lesbian." And then one day, I looked in the mirror and I said, "If I have to fight it this hard, there's no use." And then I decided. I realized that I was a lesbian.

It was about the time, or right before, k.d. lang came out. k.d. lang was my thing; and so I took a picture of her to my hairdresser and said "Make me look like this," because I wanted the right people to know. I referred to dykes then as haircut girls, when I was still in the closet, because they all seemed to have those perfect little haircuts—you'd know a dyke because you'd know what she looked like by the way she dressed and her haircut. So I figured, well, shit, if I'm gonna get myself a date—I'm an infinitely practical girl—I'm gonna get my hair cut that way so that people will know. It was very liberating because it was my little secret thing. I finally got to be something—a queer, great.

I was just obsessed with one of my teachers. It was so funny! I would write in my journal every day, and I have an entire book devoted to her. I'd save little tags from gifts she gave me. I was constantly looking for little dyke signs from her and things like that. I'd read all her books and see if there were any gay ones there. I was so crushed out on her, I'd go nuts.

The thing was, I kept worrying about . . . well . . . I wasn't sure if she was gay. But, she was living with this woman. But I think I didn't want to believe it because I really wanted to get together with her.

I would go out and try to buy clothes that my teacher would wear and things that were more feminine, because I was attracted to her, and actually it was a little ploy. I was thinking, "How would I go about getting her," which is actually the motivation for 90 percent of how I came out. It was going after a crush.

Paige

I think the first time I actually thought about being bi or questioned my sexuality was when, under the influence, I kissed a girl. I would have been thirteen—that was the summer between seventh and eighth grade. I was river rafting on the American River with some friends. We were camping, and I guess we had gotten into one of those really deep stoned conversations. I guess we started talking about how, when you're little, we used to play doctor with a cousin or whatever. I played doctor with my cousin. We just started talking from there; it wasn't a big deal. One thing led to another, and we just kissed. After that night, I think I really started thinking about it all. That would have to be the first time I seriously considered it.

Up until about a year ago, I was really heavily into drugs and stuff like that. A lot of my experiences were clouded by that, unfortunately. I think it led me to do a lot of things I don't think I would have done. But, it got me thinking about things when I was really small. You think back and ask yourself if it's predetermined or whatever. I look back on when I was seven and eight years old. I used to play doctor with my cousin, Michelle, and it was more than doctor. I definitely think it was something, but I guess I was just so bombarded by sixth and seventh grade, having to have a boyfriend and all that.

I went to summer school over in Santa Cruz. I went there because I wanted to learn more about homosexuality. I took Twentieth Century Lesbian Literature and a whole bunch of really queer-friendly classes. I came home, and I'm like, "Yep." I had a really good time; I met a lot of really great people who were really nice to me. I'd been considering bisexuality. I met a girl who really changed my mind. I'm like, "I'm in with this." I came home after my summer school session—"Decision's made." I didn't screw around with it. Now I identify myself as lesbian and have for two months short of two years, so twenty-two months, since just after my sixteenth birthday.

Todd Fay-Long

I don't really remember when I started coming out. Being gay is just an aspect of me; I just feel like there's so much more than just being gay, even though that is a big part. But then, sometimes, I feel like being gay is part of being in a big club.

Jim

I identify as bisexual and have since I was fifteen. I remember one day I was sitting at the dinner table. I was looking at food that I wanted to eat: "Do I want meat or potatoes?" I mean this speaking metaphorically. I just wanted both. It just clicked right then. Throughout the years, I'd look at men and I was physically attracted, and I'd look at women and I was physically attracted to them too. But with men, I don't have to like their attitude or anything; it's just a whole physical thing. With women, I have to make sure that they're intelligent. It's more mental with women; it's not mental with men. I've never been out with a guy but I have wanted to.

I try not to think about sexuality in general. It's just what I do. It's my life. To me, it's nothing big. It's no big deal to me. It's just another part of life. If I want to go do a gay parade one day, that's what I'll do—I'll go. I try not to plan much; I try not to plan out my life. If you have expectations and they don't turn out the way you want, you're disappointed in the end, and I don't want to be disappointed in my life.

Chapter 3

You're WHAT? Coming Out to the Family

Anthony Gomez

I was living with my grandmother before I lived with my mother. And I called my mother up one night, and I told her, "I'm gay." And she said, "Anthony, you sure this is not a phase?" I said, "No, Mom, it's not a phase." She said, "Okay, well—I've always known you were gay." But when I went down there for a visit, my mother just couldn't handle it. First, she's real okay with it, and all of a sudden, when it comes down to the real thing, she just couldn't handle it. I don't know why. And it hurt me a lot.

She put more restrictions on me after that. I couldn't bring any boys to the house or anything like that. Once, I had my boyfriend drop me off at the house, but she didn't know who he was. She thought it was just a friend. After he left, I told her that he was my boyfriend, and she just totally freaked, saying, "I don't want anybody—any boys—in my house that you're gonna be dating. I don't want you to do anything in my house. MY house!" And I said, "Sure, alrighty then." Not long after that, I left home. And so, my mother and I have a hate relationship right now. I haven't heard from her in about five months.

Adam Hardy

I came out to my mother to live to the promise I had made to my friend Kaki before our school break. This was probably the second hardest coming out I've had to do, though I knew from the outset that she'd take it well. Mom was great about it—she did go through a little period of mourning, but, more than that, she instantly became very *worried* for me, knowing about all the homophobia I'd face. These days, she's trying to find me a man. My father still doesn't know, and I don't intend to tell him. I really don't feel much of anything toward my father, and since I know he'd react badly, I don't feel any obligation to tell him. He has not earned that from me.

Alan Wiley

Before I came out to my parents, I totally knew what was going on, but they didn't know what was wrong. I was always depressed; I wasn't eating, because not eating gave me intense pain in my stomach, and I felt because I was gay, I deserved that pain. I began to thrive on pain. I just felt like I deserved it. I felt like by being a gay person that I was somehow bad. I wouldn't eat, sometimes for five days at a time. My parents really noticed that I lost a lot of weight. They also knew that I was masochistic; I would cut myself, give myself cramps, just sew myself up with needle and thread, anything to cause intense pain. They knew this was going on, and that really scared them, especially since they came from extremely fundamentalist backgrounds; My dad couldn't even play with playing cards. And here's their kid, hurting himself and enjoying it. I got to the point where I would just take out a needle and thread right in front of them, sew on my foot and rip it out, just because it was so normal for me. I would give myself a toe cramp right in front of them, and it just didn't seem like any big deal to me anymore. And one night, I came into their room; my foot was bleeding and I was crying, and I just could not handle myself. And they said, "I don't think we can help you anymore; you need to get some help."

They sent me out to see a psychiatric social worker. I told him that I was gay and that I wanted to be straight, and to do whatever he had to do to cure me. He just laughed in my face and said, "Yeah, right. You're gonna have to deal with this." That wasn't the answer that I wanted to hear. I had convinced myself over the years that I had this problem of being gay, and I had just convinced myself that there was some way to fix it, and I was gonna find that way. I used to look at straight porn all the time, trying to turn myself straight, trying to convince myself that that was what I wanted. I tried self-hypnosis to make myself straight 'cause I'd read that you could do that. I tried just telling myself that I was straight over and over again, and it just led me to hate myself because I couldn't do it. I really hated this first social worker that I went to because he just told me to deal with it, which I think was good, but he didn't tell me *how* to deal with it. He just wanted to get me out of his office as fast as he could in as few visits as possible, because it was through a really lame health care provider. So my parents ended up sending me to an independent psychotherapist who wasn't affiliated with the same health care provider.

I went to his office, and he started out by saying, "If you don't want to be here, I don't want you here. . . . I'm only going to do this if you want to do this." And I said, "That's cool; I'm with that." So I stayed there and I told him what was going on, and he was really cool with everything. At that point in my life, I was doing a lot of drugs; I was basically stoned every day, and he told me that that was totally understandable and not to worry about that. I'm glad he did that so that I could concentrate on other issues. He not only told me that it was okay that I was gay and I was still a good person but we talked about what I could do about it, how I could tell my parents, how I could come out. It was a matter of whether I wanted to come out or not. He would only do things if I wanted to do them, if I suggested them. But he helped me start dealing with the actual feelings of coming out.

The last time I talked to him was the week before I came out to my family, and I haven't spoken to him since, and that was about a year and a half ago. I really wish that I could somehow talk to him and tell him how much he's helped me and how far I've come now. At that point, the last time I talked to him, I wasn't out, I wasn't gonna go to college, and I was just gonna live in a hole in the ground for the rest of my life. I want to thank him a lot. I wish there were some way I could.

I was already out to probably ten friends at school, and I knew I was going to be coming out to my peer counseling group I was a part of at school, which was eighty people. I wanted my parents to hear it from me and not hear it from some other source. So I just sat them down one night—I made sure everyone was gone except my parents—and I said, "I need to talk to you." And they said, "About what?" And I told them that I was going to tell them something that was really important and that they should listen and not ask questions until I'm done talking. I told them that I was gay and that I did not want to be gay, but it was not a choice; and that's why I had attempted suicide before, that's why I had problems with anorexia, and that's why I had trouble with masochism. I felt like I deserved all this pain because I was gay; I'd been told being gay was wrong, but that I'd now accepted that I was gay, and I was willing to love myself for it, and I was going to stick with that, and that if they had a problem with that, I was really sorry. I reassured them that I loved them and that I just wanted to be honest with them. My mom started crying, and my dad just sat there. They realized then how homophobic they had been when I was growing up and how badly it affected the way that I felt about myself and my self-image. They said they were sorry if they'd ever said anything that had hurt my feelings, and they asked me if there was anything they could do to help me. I said, "Yeah, I smoke too; don't give me shit about it." And so they don't give me shit about smoking now.

I've never talked to my parents about whether they blame themselves for my being gay or not. I think at first, it's just instinctive to blame yourself for anything, at least in the kind of upbringing I had. So I'm sure my mother blamed herself for a while, 'cause I know she was really upset about it, and she still cries about it. I remember telling my parents before I came out to them—when I knew I was gay but they didn't—that they had been horrible parents, but it was not their fault. That it was me, not them. Basically, I said, "I'm really sorry it didn't work out; I don't hold it against you." I can't even imagine how hard that was for my mom, because my parents love me so much. I told my mom that I thought she hadn't been the right mother for me, that she'd been okay for my brother and my sister, but that she just wasn't the right mom for me, and that I was meant to be with a different mother. But I honestly don't feel anything like that anymore. I totally appreciate my mother for everything that she's done. I guess, the way that they were raising me at the time didn't go well with what was going on in my mind. They weren't really actively homophobic, but there was a lot of homophobia just in the household. I remember when my mom was teaching me that it wasn't okay to be a racist. She told me this story about how, when she was younger and she was living in this house in Michigan, back when there was blatant racism, when the civil rights era was going on, her neighbors were moving out, and their neighbors told her family to not worry because they wouldn't sell it to any black people. My mom told me, "Well, we didn't care; they could have sold it to black people, and it would have been fine with us." But then she said, "They turned around and sold it to this gay couple," as though it was such a bad thing—"This gay couple, oh, no." That's one story that sticks out so strongly in my mind because I remember hearing that story and just feeling my heart and my stomach and all my insides just drop. I just wanted to die right then. Those kinds of things really hurt my self-esteem when I was young. Growing up gay, no one really has that much high self-esteem, even in a lot of really accepting societies. But especially coming from such a Mormon/Christian/Conservative/Gay People Suck area, you just have almost no self-esteem. I'm surprised that I have the self-esteem that I do today, or even the self-esteem that I did then, going through all of that. I had pretty high self-esteem even in junior high and high school, even though I was dealing with this.

When I came out, my parents were iffy about me being gay. They really didn't like the idea. They didn't tell me that it was a phase, or anything like that, which I'm glad of, because I would have been so mad, I probably just would have left home. But, the day after I came out to them, my mom went out and bought a book called *When Your Kid Comes Out to You,* or something like that. She just tried to understand because she didn't. She told me stupid things for a while that would really bother me. I remember, she told me that she was talking to her friend, and her friend said that the only places you can meet gay people are at gay bars, gay churches, and gay bookstores. And I just laughed in my mom's face, and I told her she was really, really stupid if she believed that. I feel bad about doing that now, 'cause I realized that she was just trying to help. But they have come so far now. My mom has developed this sense of gaydar—being able to figure out who in a crowd is gay, and my dad can pick out a total closet case. It's really nice that I can feel comfortable now talking to my parents about boys. When I was growing up, I never, ever thought I would tell anyone about this. I never thought that I would ever come out to anyone. I thought it was just gonna be my secret. I'm so glad that I can be comfortable with it now and talk to my parents about it.

Eileene Coscolluela

I haven't told my parents, but I suspect they know. I do know that they know I'm involved with the gay community, but that's about it. I come from a *very* conservative family.

Dawn McCausland

The night I got back from my first support group meeting, I lied to my mother about where I'd been. And I was horrible at lying because I had a good relationship with my mother. I was not used to doing things without her knowing it. So I did a horrible job at lying about where I'd be, and then I made it worse by going out to coffee afterward, not getting home until 11:00 or 11:30 at night. She ended up trying to track me down and calling my dance teacher and doing this whole thing. So by the time I got home, she was just freaked out beyond belief, and I wouldn't tell her what was going on. I was totally scared. I think I was probably crying. Finally, we got in a fight about it. I said, "Well, I'm not telling you where I was," and this and that. And then she sat down, and she said, "I'm worried." I told her, "Well, I just went to a support group." She got all freaked out, and I know she was thinking something bad had happened. I just blurted out, "Mom, I think I'm bisexual," and I just started crying. She just stared at me, really, really confused, like, "That's it? All this stress for that? Why are you crying?" And she said, "Okay, well, I'm glad you're safe. Good night," and left it at that.

It was kind of awkward for a while. My mother is very accepting now. I think she was accepting from the beginning; but, again, it was odd for her, because I think she would have expected it a lot more from my sister than from me. She didn't understand at all what I was going through, the hard time that I had with it, how serious it was, how much it meant to me, or how much of a huge issue it was. And she didn't have any experience of how to deal with it, so she didn't know how to support me.

Eriq Chang

I come from a very traditional Asian family. In our culture, being gay is not even really spoken about. So if my parents knew, I think it would cause a lot of problems for me. There would be a lot of difficulty adjusting. Especially for my grandparents.

I'm not the type of person to talk about who I'm attracted to anyway. It's not something that I really worry about. But it is difficult sometimes. I plan on telling my parents after I graduate from high school.

I will be moving then, and I feel it's something that they should know. It's pretty grueling sometimes to think about it. They have their suspicions, I'm sure. My dad probably does, and he's already adjusting to the fact that I cross-dress for shows professionally. But, I know that if they knew that I was bi, that they would feel disappointed. I'm prepared for that.

Ernie Hsiung

One time, my mother was cleaning my room and she read a couple of letters that I wrote to friends about guys I had crushes on in high school. When my parents confronted me about this, they suggested therapy, to change myself. But instead of telling them that they were wrong about being gay that I couldn't just change myself, I freaked out. I told them it was just a phase. They believed me and left it at that. I don't know what I'm going to do about telling my parents. They're currently supporting me financially through college, so I do not want to come out to them just yet.

Kyallee Santanders

May 6, 1993 is a day that marked a rite of passage and literally scarred me for life. After coming back from a gay youth group meeting, I asked my mother if I could go to a dance that weekend. She wanted to know whom I was going with and what the dance was for. As much as I didn't want to tell her, she already suspected it was a gay dance, and I only confirmed what she was afraid to know. My mother was immediately hysterical: "How do you know? We had no clue as you were growing up! You'll never be happy. It's just a phase. Don't you know you'll burn in hell for this?" My father looked up from the TV and said, "No daughter of mine was raised to be a lesbian." Crushed, I ran to my room. My mother followed. "And what about this group you've been going to? I suppose they're all gay?" (She had assumed that it was a social group, and I never bothered to correct her.)

In the bathroom, I curled up in a corner and tried not to cry. Life was over; I wanted to leave it bravely. I took out a twin-blade razor and made two slashes down my wrist, knowing that if I cut along the vein, I'd die quicker. I watched the blood spill onto the floor, unable to feel any of it. The world had ceased to be real. Frustrated that I couldn't feel it, I poured rubbing alcohol into the wounds, but even that couldn't penetrate the fog in my head. Wanting desperately for it to be over with, I ingested 1600 milligrams of Motrin and passed out.

I woke up at 3:30 the next morning, shaking violently. I laid in bed for an hour, and then got up, put all of my gay books and poetry, all of my tapes by gay artists, and all my pictures of gay friends into a duffel bag. I got into my car, drove to school, and fell asleep in the hallway at 5:30 in the morning.

My father called for me at school and demanded that I be taken out of class to talk with him. He wanted to know why I'd taken so many things out of my room. I said I didn't trust them to not go through my stuff after last night. He asked if I was coming home; I said I wasn't. He said he was coming to get me now if I didn't promise to come home after work. After many other such threats, I said I'd be home later and hung up.

The school was inundated with social workers due to a classmate's accidental death a few days earlier. One of them approached me and suggested I join a group down the hall who was grieving the boy's death. I told him he didn't know a damn thing about me, pushed him aside, and went back to class.

He must've told the social worker about it because I was yanked out of class again. She let me call Lena, who agreed to stop by after work and take my duffel bag. I told the social worker what had happened, and she bandaged my arm properly. The only things I had found in my house that morning to deal with that much blood were a panty-liner and some tape. She wanted desperately to have me hospitalized and my wounds stitched up, but she could see that upsetting me further would be fatal.

Over the next few days, the social worker and my parents carried on a conversation about how my lesbianism was just a phase that would end once I'd been through proper counseling. I could go back to group until a proper counselor was found to help me through this "phase."

Lisa Campbell

It was after I went to the youth group for the first time that I did come out to my dad and Cheryl, my stepmother. I did it on a Wednesday. I'd planned to do it on Monday when Dad was home alone, and Cheryl would be out shopping. And then the car broke down. Dad was in a really pissed-off mood. Tuesday, he wasn't getting home till late; Cheryl was out walking and doing all this stuff. Another day passed. Then on Wednesday it was like, "I gotta tell somebody now." So, I told Cheryl. I said, "When Dad gets home, I want to talk to both of you." She was getting this look on her face like, "Oh, no, you're moving back to Louisiana, aren't you?" She didn't say that, but I could tell the look. She asked, "Well, can you tell me?" And I said, "Well, okay." She was standing up when I told her, and you coulda knocked her over with a feather after I told her. She was just stumped. She was totally surprised. My dad said, "Oh, well, I've known that for about a year." I wanted to ask, "Why didn't you ask me instead of making me go through this torment here?" He was calm.

When I told him, I got this big lecture about how I wasn't any different from anybody else and everything. And I told him, "I know this. . . . I've been studying all this stuff so I could tell you . . . in case you objected; I've been watching all those damn specials on TV." It was like studying for a while. I had to come up with all these different angles and thought of how he might object, so I could just pin him down. He caught me off guard.

A lot of people at the youth group I go to were out to their parents. They hadn't been exiled or anything. And so I thought, well, maybe I could do it too. And so I did; I took a chance, and it turned out okay. I'm not saying my dad is totally great with it. When I went to the senior boat cruise with my girlfriend at the time, people were saying that we were making out and everything on this ship. We kissed a few times, but it was not all that. He didn't believe me. He lectured me, telling me that it's wrong to have any public display of affection. That it would make straight people uncomfortable. And I'm just like, "Fuck you, you straight white Republican male." We were in rush hour traffic, in the city, and we'd only been in the car maybe a half hour, and he was just lecturing me and lecturing me. And I was disagreeing with him and trying to explain things to him. But he kept lecturing me.

I haven't come out to my mom yet. I've thought a lot about it, and I would want my mom to be at my wedding. But, I don't want to lose my brother at the same time. I have a nine-year-old brother, and he means the world to me. He looks up to me, and I don't want anyone telling him that the person he looks up to is this gross, terrible person who's a sinner, or whatever. And so, I'm really not telling my mom to protect him. I'm gonna come out in about five years probably, when he's around fourteen. I guide him every so often when I talk to him. When I talk to him alone, I'll ask him, "Hey, what does gay mean?" He'll tell me it's when a guy marries a guy. And I'll ask, "Yeah, but what about women?" And he goes, "It's the same for them." So he's got a pretty good idea. And I've told him, "Look, you know, fag, dyke, all those names, queer, they're not bad; they're only bad if someone uses them in a bad way . . . and if your friends call you that, don't go and get mad." He's still back in Louisiana, but I'm trying to guide the little guy and tell him, so that when I come out to him it's easier. So I haven't come out to my mom to protect him. My getting married is a real important thing in my life, and I'd really like my mom to be able to be there. But at the same time, I want to keep my family for a little while longer.

Mathis

In June of 1994, my grandmother was taking a trip out to see her son—my uncle that I live with now, whom she hadn't seen in a long time. I came with her, taking the bus. I very much identified with my uncle and my aunt at the time. My uncle said that if I needed a place to stay or to get away or if I wanted to come live with him that I could. So whenever I got back, I told my mom that that's what I was gonna do. I hadn't turned eighteen yet. She said that was fine. I don't know if it was necessarily that she was trying to get rid of me or if she knew that I would probably be better off here. That's when I came out to her. Actually, awhile before that, my other uncle was living at our house. He told me that he wanted me to have sex with his wife, and he told me that my mom wanted me to do it because she was afraid I was gay, and she wanted me to at least try to have sex with a woman, so she may have suspected earlier. I remember, there were Levi's ads in magazines—I don't remember which magazine it was. I remember telling her then that the guys were gorgeous in it, and she kept asking me, what, exactly, was so attractive about it. And she kept saying, "Is it their ability?" They were jumping up and doing acrobatic-type things and stuff like that in the ad. And I said, "No, I want to have sex with them." And she kept trying to sway the conversation in another direction. I think I was fourteen or fifteen then. So I just decided to give it some time, and then I told her when I was seventeen. Everybody else knew it anyway.

Michael Talis

My parents know nothing of my "gayness." As far as I know, they think I'm totally straight. I have always "played it straight" everywhere I've gone. Never have I said anything about being gay or even discussed other gay people with them. I have always defended gay rights if a current events issue comes up, but because I am such a "straight-looking" guy, never has anyone suggested that I am gay myself.

My parents would probably be the last people I would tell about being gay. This is not to say that my parents don't have open minds and wouldn't be accepting of me, but they would be the hardest people to tell.

Mary Toth

I have a tendency, when I want something to be made known, of making it really obvious. When I'm pissed off, I act pissed off. Well, I wanted it to be known that I was queer. I was desperately afraid of it, but I was starting to make hints at it. With my parents, I didn't want to just come out and say it, but I figured they'd get the clue. Actually, it was sort of a practical move. What I thought at the time was, "Well, shit, if I'm gonna get a girlfriend, I'm gonna want to take her home with me." If I'm gonna be taking girlfriends home with me, my parents had better know.

Well, I was getting in a series of fights with my mom because I actually got a B-minus on something, and I was drinking lots of scotch and being generally unhappy. I mean, literally, if I got a C, I would expect to have both my parents gang up and give me the lectures from hell. Basically, I got the "Oh, you're stupid, you'll drop out of high school, get pregnant, and only work at Burger King for the rest of your natural life unless you shape up, blah, blah," speech. Anyway, I was having a fight with my mom about my grade, and she yelled something like "Just because you think you're a fucking dyke!" or something like that—that was the first indication that my mom was getting the clue. And I'm thinking, "Okay, great," but I couldn't really tell from the context whether she was just saying that to jab at me or whether she was saying it because she generally didn't agree with it.

So later on, I came out to my dad. We were driving home from high school—I have the perfect timing. We're driving past the McDonald's—I remember very vividly—and I said to my dad, "You know, I think I have a big crush on my music teacher." And he said, "Yeah, I thought I was gay once, too." And I thought, "Great." And that was really all that he said about it. Then later on, he would do things, like go to the city, and bring me home a copy of, oh, *Outlook*, because it had a picture of Jodie Foster on it—this is a big acceptance thing for me. I had made it real apparent that I had a major crush on Jodie Foster. My parents started accepting I was gay when they saw the pictures of k.d. lang and Jodie Foster plastered all over my wall. I had Jodie in her kick-boxing outfit, Jodie in an interview.

In their own way, my parents were fairly accepting. They would ask questions about it, and they wouldn't say much about it. My dad would tell me about the latest queer thing, and he'd buy me queer books, and they'd take me out to queer bookstores. So, they were kind of at a level of participation.

My first relationship sort of enlightened me. Being with Anjie in DC took me out of my home situation for over a week solid. Then coming back home, I saw a lot of what was going on with my family. I realized it was a very unhealthy situation for me to be in. It didn't have to do with them rejecting me because I was a lesbian per se. They wanted to control me, and I didn't want to be controlled.

By the time I got my second girlfriend—my first girlfriend's ex-girlfriend—I don't know how I pick 'em; I was just young and dumb. I'd already planned on leaving home. I just didn't know where and when and what the logistics were going to be. I was polite; I left good-bye notes; I gave people presents. It wasn't like I did the thing unplanned, and it wasn't like I just said, "Oh, fuck this; I'm just pissed off at my parents; I'm leaving."

I ran away to my girlfriend. And that was kind of a bad situation. It turned out to be not much better than living at home. But I lived in abject poverty for a while, so I got to see another side of the queer culture; I started hanging out a lot in the Castro because the girlfriend worked as a stripper. For better or for worse, I got to see a lot of the Castro culture.

Paige

I shared it with a lot of my friends first, my really close friends. And then, end of July, I told my mom. I took her to a place that was really special to me; it's called the Rose Garden, in San Jose. I brought lunch, and I was just gonna talk to her. She was the person I expected to get the most support from. At this point, my brother already knew. I had told my brother. So my mother and I sat down. I started talking to her about the classes I was taking, and I said, "You know, I'm not taking biology this summer. I know that's what you thought you paid for, but I went to take some literature classes that I think I'm very interested in." She asked, "Well, what did you take then? Did you take Eighteenth-Century Literature?" I said, "No, not exactly. I took Twentieth-Century Lesbian Literature." And she said, "But why?" I explained to her that, over the process of the summer and before that, I was thinking that I was bisexual, and I'd met some really nice people who had given me a great introduction to the community, and that I was starting to define myself as lesbian. She just went off: "Are you sure?" I said, "Yeah." She said, "Fine, tell me; don't tell anyone else; lay all the pressure on me to tell the family." And I answered back, "I never asked you to tell them." So I was sitting in a place that's special for me—the Rose Garden—and she's looking at me. She didn't say it, but I know I could read it from her eyes: "Oh, this is just a phase; she'll get over it." She started to actually blame it on one of my good friends who is a lesbian and whom I'd been hanging out with a lot. Not so directly, but in a very indirect way. But I got it. I couldn't deal. I got up and left. I didn't want to be around her if she was gonna be negative, and she was starting to be really negative, and she was trying to place blame and trying to make me feel guilty. I went home that evening and told my sister and my father. My dad didn't say much, but two days after, we had lunch, and he said, "You know, I really love you." I think that was very supportive; it was nice to hear that from him. But, he didn't say it was okay, just "I love you." That's something that my father has a very hard time saying. He's not very good at expressing emotions. My sister sided with my mom and tried to blame it on Lynette, my friend who's a lesbian.

I was still living in the UC Santa Cruz dorms then; I hadn't moved back to my house yet, and my parents just stopped calling. They were calling me and seeing how I was doing, but they didn't call for about two and a half weeks after I came out to my mom. I called them, and they said, "Oh, we've been waiting to hear from you." I asked back, "Well, why didn't you call?" And my mom said, "Oh, we've been so busy." I moved out after that. I moved out with my friend and lived in Los Gatos.

I'd already dropped out of high school by this point. I just needed my space. I wasn't too motivated to do anything with my life, and so I decided to move out. I had some money saved up, and I lived with my friend's parents, while he was away at college. It was time for me just to be by myself and hang out. And that's what I needed, I think. It was less stressful for me 'cause I didn't have to deal with my parents. But I didn't go about it in such a graceful way. I went about it in a very destructive manner, which was something I regret now.

My relatives would flip if they knew I was gay. But the only family I really consider myself having is my mom's. I've pretty much disowned my dad's family. I haven't talked to them in going on seven years, except for a couple of ons and offs, you know, shouting matches. My dad is really cool; my mom is still kind of unhhhhhh. I said to her a couple of days ago, "I'm going over to my girlfriend's." She said, "Oh, whose house are you going to?" She does stuff like that, and I said, "I'm going to Heidi's house." And she's, like, "Who's Heidi?"

Todd Fay-Long

I don't remember exactly when I started coming out, but I joined this youth group called Positive Images; it's the Sonoma County gay/lesbian/bisexual youth group. I got a boyfriend instantly; he picked me up right away, right when I joined the group. He was older; he was twenty-five, I was sixteen. He was just really supportive of me. I went with him to this gay prom in Sonoma County called the Rainbow Prom in the middle of May. I had told my dad I was going to this high school prom. The day after the gay prom, I called my mom and I came out to her on the phone. And she was like, "I always knew . . . no big deal." Just like that, "No big deal." She was very supportive. And I said to her, "But I can't tell Dad, you know. . . . I just can't tell him." She agreed and said I shouldn't tell him.

Although she was supportive of me, I also feel like she shouldn't have said that I shouldn't tell my dad, because I should have. I did need to tell him; I was living with him then. And I was at a stage where I was out at high school and I was ready to start getting politically active and become involved with the gay community on that level, do speaking panels and go around with schools and stuff like that. So there was one night when I stayed at my boyfriend's house. I lost my virginity to him a couple weeks before that, and so I stayed at his house, and I was feeling good when I went home the next day. It was the first time that I actually spent the night there and stayed the whole night. So I went home and I was in a great mood. I guess my dad had called there and talked to my boyfriend, because I had left the number of where I was staying. He asked, "Is Steven gay?" And I said, "No." I left and I went to work, and I called my mom; I was really freaked out, but I just knew I had to tell him. I had actually planned on coming out to him that day, but this was even before he asked me if Steven was gay. I had been planning it. I thought, "Omigod, he's gonna ask me before I can even tell him!" So I called my mom and she came and met me on my lunch break; then after my lunch break, she went over to his apartment and told him that I'm gay. So he had the chance to calm down and adjust to it until I got off work.

Then, that night, my mom, my mom's husband, my dad, and myself met at IHOP, or someplace like that, and we talked. I was crying. I was really scared. My dad was being very supportive, and he was saying, "It's okay." Just totally the opposite of what I expected. My dad's girlfriend didn't come though. He said that she was mad at me because I hadn't told her and I hadn't opened up to her. But everything I would say to her in confidence, she would repeat to him. I couldn't risk telling her first. She betrayed my confidence right after that when I sat down with her and talked to her about it all, but asked her not to repeat certain things to my dad; then later I found out that she had told him things. I went to my house and I got some clothes and I went out to my boyfriend's house and hung out there for a while. Then I went down to my mom's house to stay with her.

My dad was being a little weird, saying, "Well, you don't have to flaunt it," and all this stuff. He was really just being down on me being totally *out*. I lied when I went to the Sonoma County Gay Pride Parade. I marched in it. That was my first parade. But I didn't tell my dad that I was going to it; I said I was going to some fund-raiser or something, just because I didn't want him to give me a hard time. I feel really lucky now though, in that all of my family accepts me.

Jim

Yeah, I think my parents know. They're the kind of people who wouldn't say anything to me if they knew. I haven't told them. I'm not really close with my family. When we go to family reunions, I'm usually the person who never talks or never says hi to anybody. I just say, "Can we go? Can we go home now?"

It doesn't matter. I am gonna come out to my parents whenever I feel the need to. I wish they were a little bit more interested in what I do; they're like, "Oh, how was your day? Oh, great . . . I'm going to work and going somewhere else." They just don't pay attention to me. They don't seem to care. I tried to talk to them about it, but they just don't have time for me. It's sad. I'll probably wait until they are interested in what my life is about and in what I do. They don't even ask me who my friends are or anything.

Chapter 4

Do You Have to Let the WHOLE World Know?

Adam Hardy

As my life began to center around my struggle to hide the pain I was going through, I found I had less and less to talk about with most friends, and our conversations were strained by the weight of what I wanted to say and couldn't. With my friend, Alan, it was another story—at some point, we began talking about sex (I've always been a notoriously open person), and it soon became most—all—of what he wanted to talk about. I wanted to tell him that I was gay—I *needed* to tell someone—and I realized that I was attracted to him. Alan couldn't keep a secret to save his life, and so I cut off all contact with him to eliminate any danger that might lurk there. I *couldn't* cut off contact with my best friend, Lewis—I loved him too much.

Halfway through my sophomore year, my best friend Lewis introduced me to Pat. Pat was the first person ever to set off my gaydar *loudly.* (Lewis always registered to a certain extent, and I always wondered if he was gay, too.) To make what is a long, painful story short, Pat was a deeply homophobic gay man who was severely closeted and who sought sexual encounters with straight men. I became infatuated with Pat and somehow managed to tell him in a two-hour conversation, in which I agonized over my "horrible secret," that I "thought I might be a homosexual." That was like saying, "I think I might be male. Let me go check . . ."

Some time over the summer, I came out to my friend Mary Leah, a very vocally gay-positive new friend of mine (who was, herself, bisexual). Riding on the wave of feeling from her positive reaction, I told another close friend, Erik. The funny thing is, I knew for some time that Erik wouldn't react badly and I knew, word for word, what he'd say when I did tell him: "Why the hell didn't you tell me *before*?"

So, slowly, one by one, I began coming out to my friends. Their reaction was almost uniformly positive. I learned, then, that what they tell you is true—you don't lose any real friends when you come out. And I had made certain that I was surrounding myself with real friends. For some of my friends, I was the first openly gay person they knew, and I changed more than a few opinions on the subject. Today, most of my friends, including Erik, who's known me since I was seven or eight, say that I'm totally unrecognizable from the person I used to be.

Coming out to Erik was odd because I think it saved our friendship. Suddenly, Erik and I found we could talk endlessly without ever running out of things to say, like it had opened a floodgate and we were gushing out years of things we'd wanted to say to one another. It was incredible. Erik remains to this day one of the most integral people in my life.

My life slowly changed throughout this time. One by one, I began making very strong, close friendships with people. My fear of expressing my sexuality to anyone caused me to compensate by becoming completely honest in all other areas of my life—except for my homosexuality, I'd tell anyone anything about myself. I think this and my gentle nature caused certain types of people to gravitate toward me, and it was much to my amazement my junior year when I suddenly realized that I had a lot of friends. When I came out to people, I realized that I could be completely without fear because I had nothing left to hide. It was a good feeling.

People have tended to come out around me. Seems like it just takes one good, confident gay role model to make people feel comfortable coming out. I know that that's what I really needed a long time ago, and never got. My friend Steven came out forty eight hours after meeting me, and his friend Andrew shortly after that. Lewis seems to finally be coming to terms with himself. Several other people have come out only to me. I've also discovered that when you're out of the closet, you don't hear half the insensitive remarks you hear when you're in the closet. You also learn not to care what people say behind your back.

I'm now what you would call "pretty much out." I perpetually wear my freedom rings in Massachusetts and Alabama. I've discovered that people see what they want to see, and most homophobic people wouldn't know a freedom ring if it bit them on the bum (this is how I can wear them around my father). Anyone who asks, or even hangs around me long enough, will know that I'm gay. My sister, who's gay positive, has seen me with the rings on, so I assume she knows by now. I don't interact with most of my family enough for them to figure it out, and I don't think I'd tell them if they asked.

Alan Wiley

I was seventeen years old when I came out to my family and to my high school. I came out to myself when I was about thirteen or fourteen, between junior high and high school.

I remember I had the interesting experience of coming out to some of my friends before I came out at high school; I had a lot of close friends that were very involved with being Christian or very involved with being Mormon. I remember I was somewhat of an anti-Christian for a while in high school because I thought that all Christians hated fags, and I was big into being a fag then, so I would hate the Christians back. I decided that I would take a risk. One of my good friends is a Mormon convert; his family is not Mormon, but he is, and he's really into being Mormon. I just went out with him one night and decided to talk to him about it. I told him how I felt different, how I felt like I was standing out. I didn't feel like I was even involved with my friends; I couldn't relate to my friends, just because they weren't experiencing the same things that I was. And he said, "Oh, yeah, I feel like that sometimes, too." And I said, "No, you don't understand. I really feel different; I really feel like I'm different from everyone else." And he said, "Oh, I've felt that way before too." And I said, "Kurt, I'm gay." And he was taken aback. But the way he reacted to that situation really changed the way I felt about Christians. He said that I was okay, and he gave me a hug, and he said that he was going to treat me the way Jesus would have treated someone in this situation. And I found that very commendable—that really changed the way I felt about Christians.

I'm glad I had the opportunity to share this with Kurt, because not only did that change the way that I felt about Christians but that changed the way that he felt about gay people. So we could both make each other understand where each other was coming from, and we're still great friends. I'm glad I know him. I also came out to lots of other Christians and Mormons, one-on-one. I was always afraid of coming out to people I knew had made homophobic remarks in the past. That was difficult for me.

Occasionally, my straight male friends would flirt with me. But that, to me, was more of a sign that they were comfortable with my sexuality and that they didn't care, that it was no big deal; they could just flirt with me, and they didn't care what people thought of them. That means so much to me, when a straight guy will put his arms around me and tell me that he loves me. It means so much to me because I had to conquer so much homophobia within myself; if I was straight, I don't think I could have done that with a gay person. I think I would have really had a hard time with that, and I have so much respect for these guys 'cause they can do that. I don't even think they know what it does for me. It makes me so happy.

One of my very best friends, Kyle, had made homophobic remarks out loud in class before. I was going to be coming out to the whole school, but I wanted him to hear it from me and not from someone else. So I sat him down one day when we were in class, and I said, "Kyle, there's something I really, really need to tell you, and I'm afraid to because I don't know how you're gonna react." He said, "Just tell me." So I said, "You know, I'm gay. I know you've made homophobic remarks in the past, and I hope it doesn't affect our friendship or anything." And he said, "Oh, don't worry about it. My aunt's gay, and I've been trying to stop making homophobic remarks. . . . I've really been trying, but . . . you being gay is totally fine with me." He's the greatest guy. I totally love Kyle. He's awesome. One thing that made me feel especially good was when we were out driving around in his car. Some guy cut him off and he said, "Oh, you faggot." And then he put his hand over his mouth fast. And I said, "Well, you know, that's okay." And he's like "Whoops!" And I said, "Oh, don't worry about it. It was just a joke, right?" Then he said, "No, I totally forgot. I'm so sorry." "Oh, don't worry about it; I understand." I told him. "No, it's not okay; you don't understand; It's not okay; that's not okay." I said, "Don't worry about it, Kyle. I forgive you." He's like, "No, it's not okay. You have to be mad at me." And I just said, "Okay, if you do it again I'm gonna cut your balls off, so don't do it again." And he said he felt better. That really showed me that he loved me for who I was and that my being gay didn't play into our relationship. Just the fact that he felt so strongly about not being homophobic had a big effect on me.

I'm a freshman at San Francisco State University right now, and I'm living in the dorms, and just skating through school, having a blast. All my friends in college know I'm gay, and I'm happy about that. Ever since I came out in high school, I've been very, very out. Being out is something that's really important to me. I know when I was closeted I didn't know any gay people, and if I would have known a gay person, I would have felt so much better about myself, and I would have felt like I had a role model. And therefore, I am as out as I can be, just 'cause I want other people to realize that you don't have to fit the gay stereotype to be gay.

You can be butch and be gay and don't have to flame all over the place. Every stereotype just doesn't matter because it doesn't fit. I called my dorm roommate before I moved in with him and I told him that I was gay just so there wouldn't be any problems. He's less of a homophobe than I am. One time, in the dorms, I got called a fuckin' faggot. I wasn't really upset about it 'cause I was used to it from high school. But my roommate got so mad, he was ready to kill someone over it. He was so upset that someone called me a fag. My roommate is the coolest guy in the world. I love my roommate.

Eileene Coscolluela

My ex-boyfriend and my friends in high school, at least my close friends, know. My current boyfriend knows that I am attracted to women, but since I don't really label myself as a bisexual, he doesn't identify me as being bisexual, just as being attracted to women (and I do have a type of woman!). My current friends know that I have an attraction to women but I don't consider myself a bisexual.

My friends in the past and high school know because they were a part in my own coming-out process. It was through their acceptance of it that I could come out very easily and accept my feelings. My current boyfriend knows because I talked to him about it, and with my current friends, it's more of a passing joke. I've always been very direct with my friends in the past so I just outright told them that I had feelings for members of the same sex. It's been so long ago (in my mind) that I can't remember much of it. All I remember was them being very accepting.

My current boyfriend reacted in a very nonchalant manner when I told him that I fantasized about women. I brought it up when we were discussing sexual issues, fantasies, things like that. My current friends have it as a running joke that I'm so open, and when I just mention, "Oh, I think that woman is attractive," but that's about it.

Dawn McCausland

I came out to my best friend, who was questioning her sexuality at the time. She was wondering if she was bi and having a lot of feelings for women. I remember the conversation very vividly because I was totally freaked out when I told her. I don't want you to hate me." Looking back on it, it was really silly; here she was, talking to me for like two or three weeks about her feelings for these women and how she's starting to define herself as bisexual and this whole thing, and I'm sitting there going, "Well, are you gonna think differently of me? Is this gonna change our friendship?" and "I'm not attracted to you." But, I had such a messed up idea of reality. I felt like everyone was gonna hate me.

I have another vivid memory about coming out to other people. I was in peer support that year; it was my sophomore year in high school, and that was the beginning of my coming-out process, the hard part. I was starting to come out in my peer support class, and I went to a workshop in Santa Rosa with a bunch of high school kids. We were working on prejudice, and we had done a line experiment where they would name a category and you would cross the line and face the rest of the group, and everybody would be silent and see how it felt to be on either side of the group. And we'd go through religions and races and single parents, alcoholics, and all of that. And one of the categories was if you define yourself as gay, lesbian, bisexual, or have a family member who does. I just remember crossing the line and being so terrified. I don't remember anyone stepping over the line with me. All the other ones I remembered very vividly, which friends came over with me and what it felt like.

It was just like this spotlight was on me, and I just blanked out. I was totally freaked out. It's funny, because the buffer was there. I could have easily said, "Oh, well, I have an uncle who's gay," or something stereotypic like that. But it was just that suddenly I knew inside that I was defining myself that way.

When I moved out into my own place, I was interviewed by this totally anonymous roommate. We got through everything, and everything was fine, and we got to the end, and my heart's pounding a little bit because I've met her boyfriend, and I'm, like, "Okay, well, the only problem I see is that I'm gay; I'm a lesbian, and if you have a problem with that, then this isn't going to work between us because I'm very out." She just looked at me and she smiled and she said, "Oh, that's no problem; I'm bi."

Eriq Chang

One of my closest friends knows, and he's pretty comfortable with it. I have a friend Don who knows and I had a boyfriend Mark. And a teacher knows. And my counselor. Basically, if you're gonna ask me what my sexuality is, I will tell you. So I'm sure a lot of people know at school.

Ernie Hsiung

Most of the time I felt like an outsider. Because I didn't really get along with the people at my school, I looked to the church for support and soon found a group of Christian friends who went to my church. Finally, these were some people who accepted me for who I was, and I didn't feel like such the outsider anymore—of course, I didn't tell them I was gay: then they wouldn't like me anymore.

During high school, I told three people in my church group. One girl took it very well, while the other two guys accepted me as a friend, but condemned "my sin" and didn't want to talk about the feelings I had. It was okay at first, but it ended up hurting me because I couldn't tell my closest friends how I felt toward other people.

Now that I am in college, things are a little different. I live in the dorms, and I am still hesitant every so often about coming out to people because I'm afraid that they will reject me or condemn me. I guess I'm expecting what some of my friends from church did. But so far, all of my coming-out experiences have been positive, even though I've only come out to four people on my dorm floor. I've been starting to hang around more gay people also, so I am gradually coming out of my shell.

Kyallee Santanders

I told a few close friends in high school, and most of them took it well. I tend to pick very open-minded people to be friends with, so I haven't had many problems. Most of my friends now are either lesbian or gay friendly. I refuse to be friends with someone I have to hide myself from—part of being a friend is being supportive, and how can someone be supportive if they don't accept you for who you are?

Lisa Campbell

This person in my Algebra II class and I were talking about being normal, and we were both saying that we weren't normal. Somehow, I just figured maybe she was gay. So I wrote her this note, and I give her my phone number and said, "Hey, I think our secrets are the same, so give me a call and we'll see." It turned out that she's bi. She had started to realize this when she was at a summer camp and she met her first girlfriend, who was a total dyke, lives in San Francisco, and everything. So it made her come out real quick, you know. She was the first one of my friends I told.

My friend Renee kinda suspected. She knew about some poems that I was writing at the time about death and stuff. And my friend Shalyn suspected, because Renee told her. Shalyn had read one of my poems titled "Death." She copied it and then she got me to sign it. She took it to her mom and showed it, and her mom's like, "Ummm." Her mom is gay too. The first time I met her mom and her lover I suspected they were gay. The way her lover wasn't really explained when she was introduced seemed suspicious. Usually, where I come from, things are explained, and this was a fuzzy gray area.

Shalyn also took the poem to one of the counselors at school, and the counselor, from what I heard, just read it and then she just dropped it. Then, they called me into the office, and they treated me like I had done something wrong for feeling suicidal. It made me feel even worse. I was having a very good day the day that they called me in. I was pretty happy that day. They called me out of PE, my favorite class. I was playing softball. It was like, "Come on, can't you call me out when we're doing exercises or something . . . call me out of history."

They were asking when my parents got divorced and that kind of stuff. I had had some troubles with my mom in the past, and I was still having a little trouble. They thought it was just that. They didn't fish for anything else. I just went in once, and it was like, "Away you go."

Then my friend Shalyn one day just says, "I think I know what kinda youth group you're going to." She'd asked me a few times, and I'm like, "Aahhh, I can't tell you. . . . I'm not gonna tell you." I say, "How do you know?" And she says, "Well, my mom asked me and we figured it out."

Then I came out to my friend Renee and another friend, Miranda, eventually. And there were some people I wanted to tell before my senior year when I had decided to come out. But I just never got around to telling them before I went and took a female date to the senior boat cruise. I hadn't really hid it up until that point. But I wanted people to be able to really notice it, and I didn't want to be one of these people who went, "Yeah, I'm gay," only if you asked me. I wanted to be really out there. I just said, "I'm gonna come out in a real public way." I didn't even tell Evan, one other kid at my school who was out. We knew each other through mutual friends. We were standing in line for the boat cruise. Evan was in front of us, and I was introducing my date to a couple of my friends. Evan turns around and says, "Hi, I'm Evan, and your name is?" to my date. It was funny the way he did it. He was really surprised, and he was very happy that I did that. He was just like, "Alright . . . somebody else who's coming out."

When I went on the boat cruise with my girlfriend, there wasn't really any hostility. She was more afraid than I was. We were both nervous about doing it though.

If I don't come out to people, it's like they're not as good of a friend to me. But when I'm out to somebody, it makes for a much closer friendship. I'm not out at my current job. At my last job, I wasn't gonna come out until I knew some people's opinions. In fact, one of my good friends—she's a pretty good buddy of mine now—she knew when I walked in the door that first day. She could tell. Finally, she made a comment, saying some positive thing. I came out after that.

But, with the job I'm at now, I really haven't come out to anyone because I don't know any of their thoughts yet. I don't know whether I'd leave a job where I didn't feel like I was gonna be able to come out. It's not all cut and dried. It depends on the money, and if I can find another job that's gonna give me the same amount of money and satisfaction. I like being out at work. It's something easier for me to do, and it's a lot easier to come out than to hide. Right now I'm spending a lot of energy hiding. They know I have a roommate. They ask me if I have a boyfriend. "No, I don't have one," and they're, like, "Oh, well, we can go help you find one." "No, no, no, no, no!"

Mathis

I always spent the night at my best friend's house—my best friend Tory, who's a girl. And at the time, Tory knew. I told Tory that I was gay. I told her that I had a vivid dream. We always did weird stuff like tell each other our dreams. I said that in my dream there was this tall guy, with blond curly hair and bright, bright blue eyes, standing on the back of my porch, naked, with leaves all around. That's how I pretty much came out to her. After that, I just started making references to guys and stuff like that.

I got fired from a job for being out. I never really told the manager I was gay, but I told other employees. My boss had told me I needed to be more butch. I answered, "Well, it'll be hard, but maybe I can do it." I was working with a lesbian, and we were talking about it and then it ended up, two days after Christmas, both of us got fired. It was only us two.

Michael Talis

None of my friends know about me being gay. This is an issue I have really been grappling with for a while. I knew that I needed to talk to someone about this, otherwise I was going to burst, but telling someone about being gay was a chore in and of itself. Luckily, I found the Net newsgroups on-line.

I've written several notes on the newsgroup about my friend situation—it's an interesting one. I have many friends, both male and female. I play a very straight, normal kinda guy. In fact, I've gone out with two or three girls over the past year or two. My guy friends talk about the normal teenage guy things: girls and sports. The discussions of girls can get pretty crude, as you may well know, and saying, "Well, Paul, I'd really like to do it with you more than I'd like to do it with Charlotte" is a little out of place to say the least.

My friends and I will often make fun of other guys (not to their faces) about being a fag. There's one person in our group of friends who always gets the brunt of our fag-loser jokes. In fact, he's not gay at all, but very straight (and one of the most attractive men I've ever seen!). I think they're just jealous that he's smart, good at sports, and gets all the girls! What you have to realize here is that I'm a gay man making jokes about homosexuals with my friends so that they won't think that I'm gay. What's wrong with this picture?

I don't know of any people who are gay in my school. There's always the types where you say, "Obviously he's gay!" But, you can't rely on stereotypes, as I am not a stereotypical gay man.

I've known many of my friends for a long time, others for shorter amounts of time, but the last thing they would expect was that I was gay. One thing I spend a lot of time doing is going through each of my friends in my mind and playing out every possible reaction that she or he might have. Considering that my male friends are always under the pressure of the group to be "cool" and think of gay men as losers, I'm not quite sure how *each* of my friends thinks of homosexuals. When talking about homosexuals, you can't make the group "Eww!" a basis for judging a particular friend's reaction to coming out. In fact, one of my closest friends may be gay, but my group of friends isn't too supportive of homosexuals, so I don't think anybody would come out. Any homosexual's greatest fear about coming out is that they'll be rejected by friends, family, or the public in general. But what other people have been trying to convince me is that there are more homosexuals than I think. So even if you do come out and get rejected, they will always be someone else there who knows how you feel and would love to be your friend.

Paige

It was a very "in" thing at my high school to be bisexual. Not a big deal. It wasn't like you'd go home and tell your parents you're bisexual, but it was no big deal with friends. I can just remember conversations where it was said, "Oh, bisexuality is really cool." By women though, not among men.

Todd Fay-Long

Well, I have a lot of friends. I know a lot of people because I've lived in the same small town and the area around it for a long time. Well, I was out to some of my friends; I had come out to some of my friends in Petaluma as bisexual because a lot of my friends were coming out as bisexual. It was acceptable with them for me to say that. So I was out, but only with a few people, and not with any of my friends. I knew I was gay, but I just thought it would be easier to say bisexual because it was just more acceptable.

Right now, I'm out to all of my friends as gay. All my friends are cool with it. I didn't lose any friends when I came out to them. I have different groups of friends; I have my friends whom I went to high school with, who are all straight girls. I've gone to two high school parties in the last month, and I never went to high school parties when I was in school, so that's kind of a trip. I am just myself. I don't try to act all, "grrrr," drinking beer, that kind of thing. So they've all been cool with it. Then I have my friends who are kinda punk who are cool with it, too. And then I have my gay friends, from my youth group, and, of course, they're cool with it.

I remember coming out to one of my best friends. With most of my friends, there was never a point that I sat down and said, "I'm gay." But with this one friend, a friend from when I went to Rancho Cotati, I'd always acted straight. So I remember, she's the only friend that I ever sat down with and said, "I'm gay." It came as a surprise, but she was really cool with it. She just gave me a big hug, and she said, "It doesn't matter, you know, that's cool; we can scam on guys together now." But with most of my other friends, I was just always kinda out to them; I would just start talking about thinking that guys were fine and that kind of stuff. Going to clubs and that kind of thing. And I'd keep saying those things, and I'd let my friends figure it out.

Jim

I haven't really told anybody. If somebody wants to know what I'm about, they have to ask me. It's not like at an interview; they ask you, "Are you queer?" I'd say yes if they did, though. I'm not scared of it at all. If they can't handle it, too bad.

Whoever bothers to find out who I am . . . all my friends who I really care about end up knowing. It wasn't like a specific date that they knew, it would just build up to it, and then they just ask me one day, and if they ask me, I would tell them the truth. They were curious about it, but they're a little bit skeptical about it; if they can't get used to it and if they don't feel comfortable around it, that's their problem, not mine. I've had to deal with a lot of losses with friends and stuff. But I don't let it get to me. That's their problem if they don't want to get to know me. I think I'm a pretty nice person.

My old girlfriend and I used to go out with this other couple, Summer and Candle, and they were both bisexual. Cathy hangs out with people who are gay and straight, just everybody. She thinks it's fun to have me walk along with her and say, "Oh, that guy's cute." She was just great. But we're not together now.

I still have feelings for girls unfortunately. I had to go through a long period of time where I was just like, "Who cares if I want both?" You obviously can't have both at one time or at least that's not what I want. The next person I go out with will probably be a guy, though. I don't know. I haven't tested the waters there. But I know I'm attracted to guys, and I can be in love with anybody. I can be in love with a girl or a guy.

Chapter 5

Condemned or Redeemed? What Does Your God Think of All This?

THE CHURCH, SCHOOL HALLS, AND THE INTERNET

The shaping of sexual identity is such a social process. So much of the frustrations experienced by queer and questioning youth come not from their own misgivings or confusions about their feelings but rather the conflicting dissonant messages they receive from the cultural institutions they traditionally turned to for guidance.

Chapters 5, 6, and 7 examine the common and not-so-common cultural institutions that have come into play to lesser and greater extents, depending on the person speaking. Spirituality, school environments, and the Internet have had varying effects on the youth in this collection. For some, these institutions have served as backdrops to their understandings of themselves and their sexual identity. For others, the impact has been more substantial.

Spirituality, particularly in the United States, tends to be found in more traditional structures of religious worship, most commonly as Judeo-Christian religions. Whether one actually practices these beliefs or not, one is likely to encounter the morals and standards of these belief systems, as they permeate our society at many levels. As several young people describe, this encompassing value system often plays like a never-ending record telling them they are evil for who they are and what they desire.

No less torturous is the daily heterosexism and harassment most young queers face in predominantly hostile school environments. Schools tend to represent everything young people are expected to model, as they are groomed to take their place in society as fully participating adults. Gender roles and (hetero)sexuality are cemented through the molding experiences of school dances, high school parties, and so on. There is arguably no stronger bastion of conformity and ramrodding of mainstream normality than high school, where all youth are expected to get decent grades, find their first love, and move on to the responsibilities of adulthood in a quiet, orderly fashion. This environment is violently antagonistic toward anyone—queer or otherwise—dabbling with the norm, pushing against what one is expected to be. It is here that social pressures to fit in and seem straight are at their strongest for most queer youth.

It is not surprising that several of the young people in this selection describe their school experiences with rage and frustration. Yet several of them were able to turn a bad situation into a learning experience for those around them (staying alive and in one piece in the process). It is a sad comment on our current school system that an overwhelming number of the young people in this collection describe their school experiences as no less than a living nightmare.

Of all the external impacts discussed in this section, I think the Internet as a social space is perhaps the most unique and holds the greatest potential for radically altering the way young queer people construct and assert a queer sense of self.

In my efforts to find queer youth for my graduate studies of queer youth identity, I turned to a place rumored to be anonymous, equalizing, and unregulated by bastions of homophobia—I searched the Net. At a point when their age makes entry into the queer world (to say the least) problematic and in an era when mainstream society assumes they are no more than "confused," the virtual world of the Internet serves as a dynamic location for young queer cultural reality.

When I began my investigations, I presumed, as many do, that the Net was an end in itself; I thought these youth might cling to the Net as their only safe haven to exist as queer, but confine this identity to this virtual space. Quite to the contrary, queer youth use this medium as a means to a very specific end: to find and make contact with others like themselves, and by their own testimonies, this contact often extends beyond their terminals.

Queer youth do not come to on-line spaces to be lost or escape but to be found by others they think might be like themselves. So, for these youth, is virtual space any less significant than "real" space? I would argue that such superficial distinctions of space are distracting us from observing the many contexts, both on- and off-line, in which individuals—youth, in this case—define and redefine their identities.

Spirituality, school environments, and the Net all act as social contexts and backdrops to the process of identity development and growth young queers experience and live with every day. No matter how supportive or neutral one's other immediate surroundings (home or friendship circle) may be to the expression of queer sexual identity, these three places are bound to add an element of unpredictability to the mix. These contexts embody and mirror society's attitudes and actions taken toward queers in the United States today and, as such, with the noted exception of the Net, are often unaccepting and difficult to endure.

* * *

Anthony Gomez

My family are really heavy Catholics. My aunts know that I'm gay. My aunt, the one that I lived with, knows, but my uncles and my grandparents don't. The reason why my uncles and my grandparents don't know is that my whole family's very Catholic. I want to tell my grandmother, but I'm just so afraid of putting her in the grave. I don't want to. Religion has affected my life, but I really don't believe in religion because it's just of no use to me right now.

Adam Hardy

The Metropolitan Community Church was recently constructed in Huntsville, where before it had just been an office building, and there was a small uproar among Huntsvillian conservatives against it. Religion and I have never gotten along—I've never been able to reconcile my homosexuality, which is perfectly natural and God-given to me, with popular religion's problem with homosexuality. I went through a long period of anger with God before I found a sort of spirituality sans religion. I think that my homosexuality has given me a unique necessity to question religion, and I feel better for having done so, because my beliefs are based now on concepts that I've thought long and hard over.

Being gay has also imbued me with a series of bigotries that I'm learning to get over. Over the past few years, I've had to take down carefully constructed defensive bigotries in myself—Christians are *not* necessarily bad, Republicans should *not* all be shipped off to an island together, etc. I've also had to get over biphobia I picked up along the way and accept that bisexuals *do* exist and their sexuality is just as valid as mine. Took me a while to learn that being gay doesn't automatically mean you're not prejudiced.

Alan Wiley

As far as from the book's position, the RLDS (Reorganized Church of Jesus Christ of Latter-Day Saints) church is not antigay. They're not necessarily really progay either; they're just gay neutral. There is a gay group within the church that my mom keeps trying to get me involved with. But I feel like until that church starts marrying gay people, I'm not gonna be a part of it. Until they do what Jesus would have done in that situation, I'm not gonna believe it. They're not doing what they should be doing. But the religion itself doesn't really think gay people are any better or worse than anyone else.

Ernie Hsiung

Six years of church and all your friends being Christian does rub off on you. Through high school, I had learned that while loving another guy wasn't bad, having sex with him was. I'm not so sure if I believe that anymore. Some of it has gone away after going to college. . . . I've told most of my friends that these are my years to "discover myself," and they've taken the fact that I haven't gone to church at Davis rather well.

Kyallee Santanders

I left the Roman Catholic Church shortly after coming out, and my sexuality just added fuel to the fire. . . . I'm now pagan and much happier. I figure that the powers that be made me this way, and They don't make mistakes. Besides, why should I be condemned for who I love?!

Lisa Campbell

When I was a freshman in high school and first figuring things out, the reason I was very suicidal was because I was raised Southern Baptist. Southern Baptists strictly believe that if you're gay, you're going to Hell. I spent a couple of years thinking, "I am going to burn in Hell." I was very suicidal. I just wanted to be out of that pain. That was my freshman year. I had made some cuts on my wrist and stuff. Some of 'em were rather deep. And I cut both ways. My dad saw it one time. He finally cornered me and asked me what the marks were and I said, "Well, I was playing basketball, and the girls I was playing with had really long fingernails, and they're mean; they just claw you." He believed it. I'm thinking, "What kind of idiot are you?" A lot of the cuts had almost healed by that time, so it didn't look as bad, but come on!

I kinda ignore my Southern Baptist upbringing. I've decided that's the way they believe, but I don't believe the same way. I don't believe God is a bigot. So I haven't really gone to a church, and I haven't really figured out everything that I believe. I do, however, still pray and I do use Jesus' name when I pray, so that's definitely part of my beliefs. I don't go to a church, though. When I was in ninth grade, a freshman, I wanted to kill myself because I didn't want to let my family down, but also because I didn't want to let myself down in the eyes of God. So that was a big issue for me. When I overcame those feelings, it got a little easier, but it took me a very long time before I would sit down and think about my beliefs. I had a hard time with religion because it fucked me over.

Mathis

When my stepfather was younger, he was actually studying to become a priest. He told me things that were wrong—it's wrong to be gay and all kinds of stuff like that. That's how I was influenced by religion. My mother was never religious. I do believe in God now. I don't believe in the Bible. I can't believe in the Bible, or else I'm going to Hell. I believe there's an afterlife. I don't know whether it's Heaven or Hell, but religion never really affected me that much. For a little while, I was thinking, "I can't be gay, I can't admit I'm gay, because then I will be going to Hell."

Now, to me, Heaven is on earth whenever you're feeling extremely happy about something, and Hell is whenever you're hiding, whenever you're in the closet, whenever we can't feel honest with people. Honesty is a really big issue with me. I've always been this open book to all my friends, and some of them say that the most attractive feature about me is the fact that I'm brutally honest about everything. I don't know. It's kind of unusual, because that's how I end up shocking people the most, by telling them the truth.

Michael Talis

My dad is Jewish and so am I, technically. I am a little frustrated with the religion because I don't really see the need for praying to a God, a Rabbi, etc. What I prefer is Quakerism. In Quakerism, there's what's called Meeting for Worship. We're required to go at my school, Westtown, but I've gotten used to it and now appreciate it. At Worship, everybody sits on benches in a room and stays quiet. There is no preaching, no music, no noise. If you feel the urge to tell the community what is on your mind, you stand up and talk about it. Meeting for Worship is not a place for business, but just a time to think. So as you can see, Meeting for Worship doesn't make you talk to one god, listen to any sort of dogma, or, for that matter, stay awake. It's a very *open* service, which is why I prefer it. Not believing in a god above who is supreme myself, I welcome Meeting for Worship as an alternative to "praying."

Chapter 6

Kids in the Hall: What Is It Like at School?

Anthony Gomez

I go to school in Hayward. It's strictly hell. The students are so close-minded. Right now, some of my closest friends know I'm gay. They're not all so afraid. They're just like, "We know this." All the reactions I've gotten have been, "We know this, Anthony." They know me already. I am a queen.

A lot of people pick on me at school and pick fights with me. At school, I've had fag spray-painted on my locker, gay porn pinned to my locker, and death threats on my locker too. I had three boys suspended the other day for harassing me, saying they're trying to pick fights with me, calling me a faggot, a queer, and all that stuff. I finally just got pissed and I was about to fight 'em, but I said, "Look, you want me to show you what a real queer can do?" So I went to the principal's office and told her. They were there threatening to beat me up after school if they got suspended. Well, the principal said, "We'll see who's gonna threaten who." I was so happy.

Other faculty members at school are supportive, too. Both of the principals know I'm gay. My music teacher knows I'm gay because I'm in choir. And the counselor knows I'm gay. It's pretty cool; they're accepting. This is the first time they ever really had a gay young person go to their school at age fourteen. It blows their minds. They're really cool there.

I think there are some kids at school that may be gay or lesbian, but they don't want to come out in school. I think we need to have a gay group in our school. Basically, I'm almost completely out at school. I am such a queen you cannot miss me, okay? But I'm sick and tired of everybody asking, "Are you gay? Are you a faggot? Are you a queer?" I'm like, "Shut up!" I'm sick and tired of all these questions.

Adam Hardy

I started off in kindergarten in an expensive private school. What amused me was that the computer skills I learned there got me through all of my middle school computer classes, which I think says something very interesting. As of first grade, I went to public school, where I discovered that school was a Bad Thing. I never really socialized well—I was too open, all emotion and trust and no defense. I daydreamed, I stuttered, and in general, I didn't get along well with other children.

High school was torture, pure and simple. I've always been sort of effeminate, and every day felt like a struggle to hide what I was thinking from everyone else. I really don't know how I survived it all. It wasn't simply my sexuality, of course, but that was what was primarily on my mind. My high school, Lee High, was full of stereotypical rednecks, and "fag" was *very* commonly used, though never to my face. I remember sitting in class and quickly looking down at my papers every time someone said "gay" or "fag" because I was afraid people would see the expression of surprise or pain on my face and figure it out. At that point, of course, life would be over. To make matters worse, all my friends were scattered across the five high schools in the city, so I had few people to turn to for support.

The terrible headaches I got as a kid became less frequent when my senior year began, but I was restless and unsatisfied with school. It occurred to me that few well-adjusted gay men would stay in my hometown of Huntsville, Alabama, for long and that I wasn't likely to find anyone there. Classes weren't challenging me, and the homophobia at my school was making me miserable. I was doing well—winning writing awards, running the newspaper and literary magazine—but I felt like my time in Huntsville was over.

That's when I discovered Simon's Rock. Three hundred students; intense and personal academics; extremely liberal (I'd heard there was *no* homophobia); and it rescued students out of high school, not requiring a diploma. Best of all, it was in the North. So I did one of the scariest things I've ever done, next to coming out, and applied. I got accepted, dropped out of high school halfway through my senior year, and flew off to Massachusetts to go to college.

Alan Wiley

I didn't really have a good environment in high school to come out. The thing that got me to come out was that in my peer counseling group, we dealt with ten subjects, and one of the subjects was sexuality. When I was a junior, I was out to maybe two people in my high school. And that's when we first discussed that issue. A lot of the peer counselors that I was with would discuss the issue, but they really wouldn't take it seriously and constantly told fag jokes and everything in front of everyone. And here I am, the little closet fag, sitting here listening to this. It really made me feel bad. So I decided at that point, I would start to speak out as progay, even though I wasn't identifying as gay and I wasn't out at the time. When we were discussing the issue, I made a huge speech about it, and I think that affected a lot of people, knowing that it mattered to some people. I think their general impression was, "Oh, it doesn't matter because people really aren't gay." What I think teachers could do is just make gay people visible and not be afraid of that.

When I was in history class, I'd be learning all this history, and I almost felt like it didn't even apply to me because I didn't relate to it; it wasn't about my people—these people hadn't been through the same experiences that I had; this was someone else's history. I still learned it and everything, but there would be times when I'd know a certain person in history was gay, and they'd make them out to be straight in this history book. That really bothered me a lot; it made the kind of people that I could relate to invisible, so I couldn't relate at all. What I did like was when teachers would bring up the fact that this author is gay or whatever, and we would discuss it. When homosexuality would be talked about in an objective way and not looked down upon, it made me feel as if I could approach that teacher. We had the first gay city council member elected in San Diego, and not one of my teachers talked about it. The only reason I knew was because I was down in Hillcrest, the gay area in San Diego, and the news was everywhere. Schools need teachers that present a gay positive image, teachers that don't let kids get away with calling each other fags in class, teachers that don't hesitate to talk about gay issues. Treat homophobia just like you would racism. Racism is not accepted any longer, and homophobia shouldn't be either. I didn't approach any of my teachers about being gay until I didn't care anymore.

I had some liberal teachers. I came out to a lot of my teachers before I came out to the school. I really hold it against some of them that they told me not to come out. I only had two teachers encourage me to come out, and I told them that that was what I wanted to do. I don't think I'll ever forget one teacher in particular, my AP English teacher. I told him that I was gay and that I was seriously thinking about coming out, and he said it was a bad idea, that I shouldn't do it. And this is for you: "Fuck you! I'm out! I did it and I lived through it."

When I came out in high school, it was kinda weird because I was a good student. I got good to okay grades; I was really involved. I played the tuba and was tuba section leader for two years; I was in peer counseling for two years—I was a group leader in peer counseling, I did all the right things. So, when I came out, it was like, "How can this guy that does all the right things be gay?" And I had been asking myself the same question for a long time.

As soon as I came out to one of my classes as a class project—about fifteen minutes after the class was over, we had a break, and by my next class everyone knew, they'd heard. It was the hottest piece of gossip around. It was pretty wild. My school was a large school, probably about 26 or 2,800, something like that. It was so strange that everyone knew.

Initially, people were kind of in shock, and so I didn't get much reaction. But once it started to sink in to people, I started to get more reactions. I would either get support from someone or I would be called names. I was the only out person in my high school at that point. I remember walking down the hall being called "Tinkerbell" and "fairy" and "faggot" and all that kind of stuff. It got really bad, to the point where I had to be escorted from class to class because people would follow me. At lunchtime, I would go sit in a room just to eat my lunch by myself, and people would open the door just to look at me, like I was some sort of spectacle to them. I would get threats of violence and spit on.

I wanted to go to prom with a guy very badly, just to show everybody that I could, but my boyfriend already had a date with a girl. So I went into Gay Youth Alliance and asked everybody, "Who wants to go to prom?" I ended up going with this guy I didn't even know who went to San Diego State. By the time prom happened, we had met three times. I only saw him once again after that.

Going to prom with a guy caused a lot of problems because people didn't like the idea of me "ruining" their prom by coming with a guy. But I did it anyway, and I got death threats before I went to the prom, pretty much from the entire lacrosse team, the football team, and the wrestling team. I had a meeting with the principal of my high school about it. I just said, "Look, I'm getting all these threats." And he said, "We'll take care of it." We thought we were gonna have police protection when we went, but we didn't; It was fine, though. We had a great time. I doubled with a lesbian couple, one of whom went to my school. It was so liberating to stand there, slow dancing with a guy in front of all of these people that I had grown up with. People were staring at us with their jaws on the floor in disbelief. I would just smile at them. The photographers gave us funny looks when we went to get our pictures taken. It was really neat to know that I was the first one at my school to do this. It was my own little revolution, and I was proud to be able to stand up for myself and not let other people's opinions and threats stop me from doing what I wanted to do so badly. It was absolutely incredible. I'd do it again in a second.

Dawn McCausland

I was very sensitive to everything that went on at school, I had a totally messed up sense of reality. I felt like everyone was gonna hate me. I took everything very, very personally. High school was very abusive because of that. All the "faggot" and "dyke" comments affected me a lot, and I felt helpless because I didn't have any other options until I started going to a support group. That group totally changed things. When I saw happy gay people, functioning gay people, youth that were talking about sex and their significant others in normal terms, like girlfriend, boyfriend, I could relate to that. They would do normal things like go out and go dancing, and they'd go out to dinner, and hold hands in the street. That was really amazing.

So I went through, I don't know, about several months of just combating and dealing with it all, getting into gay culture, getting into having gay friends, being out, wearing buttons, pins, or symbols. Then

I got pride happy. And I told everybody. It started to be a really big thing. I started coming out to other family members and friends. After the summer that I started going to support group and I started really coming out and telling people, it was also the summer that I decided to leave high school, after my sophomore year.

I decided that intellectually I was ready to leave; it was pointless for me to be in high school. And I had no friends really, besides my two best friends, who were in fact leaving high school. It was totally pointless for me to stay there. I also realized that I had spent this entire summer working through all my internalized homophobia shit—not all of it because I'm not even done now—but working through it—and I was gonna go back into this incredibly abusive environment, where I would either have to sacrifice myself or put myself on the front lines and be fired at all the time. That was really hard for me to deal with, so I didn't. I decided that there was no way that I could compromise myself and go back to high school. So I left. Just like that. In about two days, I left.

I went to junior college, and I found that it was much easier to come out in junior college. People were generally either apathetic or accepting. They just honestly didn't give a shit very often. I've only had one person explicitly attack me or threaten me. I have come out in basically every class that I've been in. I was doing speeches on it, writing papers on it, discussing it when it would come up in a classroom or when something relevant to it came up. And I never really got any problems. I might get some weird looks, but it was never a problem. And I'd only have to see them for an hour and walk off campus. They really didn't care about me, and that was really conducive to dealing with coming out.

What was cool about leaving high school, though, was I got to totally reevaluate my entire life and my social scene. I basically structured my entire social life on people in my support group, making them, you might say, my gay family. I got to structure my entire social life so when I went into friendships, even if they were with straight people, it was on the table right from the beginning. I didn't have to come out to that many people. I just said, "Oh, well, this is me, and if you can't deal with it, then I don't want to be your friend. And if you can, I'd love to have you around."

Eriq Chang

In elementary school, it was very difficult because I would just be constantly called a sissy, queer, and confused. Junior high was a turning point because I sort of discovered my more artistic side rather than my feelings for other people. That was when the teasing and jokes started.

When I was a freshman, a lot of people would talk behind my back. I remember one day I was in English class, and I did this video where I had a wig on and I had lipstick on or something. It was just supposed to be funny. People didn't take it as funny. They took it seriously, "He's queer.' That was difficult for me because everyone in the class was just really a macho boy or femme girl. That was my freshman year. I could tell they were talking, and I just wanted to leave. Actually, I did leave at the end of the period, close to the end of the period, just to go to the bathroom; I didn't want to face it. That was something I'll always remember. I hated it. After I left the class, people started the rumors and stuff.

And in my sophomore year, this big rumor went around—I don't know where it started—that I went to San Francisco and sang at a gay bar and had sex, totally fucked like six different guys at once. And so I went through this sort of depression period. At lunchtime, I'd go on these walks and think about what was in my future. Was it wrong to like both boys and girls? How am I gonna deal with it? A lot of people would tell me that being bisexual is just a cover-up for being gay. If I was gay, I would simply come out and say, "I like men." But I have an attraction to both. At school, that's sort of a problem. They either think I'm one way or the other.

Basically, now that I have done drag, a lot of the jocks that used to make fun of me accept it. Or they want to go out and take pictures because they're very interested in it. I guess I could say, I sort of won a battle in high school. I don't want to sound egotistical or anything, but I feel I've sort of been a role model at school.

This one gay teacher I have really looks up to me because during high school, he would never have been able to do what I do now. I look up to him because in so many ways, he is so real. It's as if my teacher feels like he can be more open with himself with me. And he loves living alone; he loves being himself. He's forty-nine years old, but he's great because he's been able to live a perfectly content life. He acts like he's nineteen. I feel that, since I am gay, I'll able to keep my youth as he has. I look at other gay people who are his age who are just old and lazy and they feel like there's nothing to do. But he feels blessed, and that's what I like about him. He's really cool, and he's a good teacher. My freshman year, he sort of knew about me. It was funny because he wanted to talk to me. I want to go back to my freshman year and totally do things over.

A lot of people have come out to me at school. I know several people who are gay, several people who are bisexual, and ten lesbians. I would never have guessed; they just come up to me and will tell me. Telling people I'm bi has been successful for me.

Ernie Hsiung

I went to a financially troubled public school for high school, but hell, aren't all public schools financially troubled these days? It was a very diverse school, with around 30 to 40 percent of the students being black, the rest divided into whites, Asians, and some Latinos. I never really felt like I belonged with the people in my school—when I was a freshman, I was in Thespians, had a niche there, but that was gone when my father told me to enroll in computer classes.

There were always people to hang around with, but I never got close to them, and they were never close to me. I didn't need them anyway, since I had my friends from church. Of course, I had lingering crushes on various guys through high school, but I was too scared to tell myself I was gay in high school, much less tell them.

Now I go to UC Davis, and I feel a lot more comfortable about my sexuality, although I don't want to come out of the closet just yet.

Kyallee Santanders

Through most of my high school, I was pretty closeted except in the county gay youth group I went to. It was a little redneck high school; there were lots of gay jokes; there were lots of fights over stupid things. I was pretty antisocial anyway. College has been different, especially Boulder. Boulder's pretty liberal, and I've been able to meet *tons* of people. I still have occasional problems—someone tried to run me down with a 4 × 4 last year, people stare at me and yell things, and stuff gets stolen off of my door, but it sure as hell beats Falcon High and the silence.

Lisa Campbell

To give you an idea about the high school I went to, there were only a few minority students at my school: three black girls; they were all sisters. We had two Mexican girls, sisters. We had one half Japanese girl. Not a lot of diversity and open minds there.

After I came out at my senior boat cruise, I did presentations on gay youth in different classrooms where I got permission to speak. I got a pretty good response with the teachers I asked because I knew them pretty well, and they were some of my favorite teachers. I asked my favorite teachers first. I went in and I did these presentations, and I learned a lot of different skills. Being able to do class discussions and teach people and just basically answer questions in a manner that's acceptable can teach you a lot. People asked all different kinds of questions. Some of the freshmen were brave and asked questions, and the people who acted up were brave and asked me a lot of questions. There were questions like, "Do you believe in God?" "What are your beliefs in God?" "How could you do this if you knew it was wrong?" "How do lesbians have sex?" and that sorta thing. For the answer to that last question, I would write "homo" and "hetero" on the board and draw a line down the middle. Then I'd say, "Okay, name some of the things straight people do; I'll write it down, and then I'll write down if gay people do that." That's how the Pacific Center—a local gay support organization—does it.

We started doing the presentations in February. And I did about eight presentations. It's a three-day presentation. The format goes: first, we give out a background study. Or actually, first we give a survey on the first day. We give a background study. Then we answer any questions that people have put on a survey we hand out. And then the second day we have a video, and then we have discussion afterward. The second day we also pass out some short stories, have 'em read 'em, and then the next day we have a discussion. We finally came up with this little role-playing thing. It was very effective in certain classes. We'd have two volunteers. One person—we'd flip a coin to make it fair—one person had to be gay, had to be closeted; they couldn't come out during the skit. The other person was gonna tell a gay joke. The gay joke was one that I'd heard in a chemistry class the year before. The joke was, "What does gay stand for? Got AIDS yet." So this person got to feel what it was like. And then afterward we'd discuss how you think this person's feeling, what could they do, what do you think they should do. The first class I did was a senior English class. All my friends were in this class. I knew practically everybody. And one of my best friends came up and said, "I didn't really understand it before. I accepted it, but now since I've heard your presentation, I understand it. I was thinking about it the other day, and I got it. I just understood it."

And after one of my presentations, I had a student come up and come out to me. I was happy that she came out. She was asking for some more information. So I told her, "I'll take you to the new youth group." So the day we were supposed to go, she couldn't do it, or whatever. A week later or something, I said, "Well, you want to go to a movie in the Castro; I'll show you around there." And so we went to The Castro and we saw *Bar Girls.* I really liked that movie. It was funny. I laughed the whole way through it. She knew I had a girlfriend at the time, and she got the wrong idea, and she grabbed my hand on the way out of the theater. And I'm like, "Oohhh, damn!"

I was pretty sure that some of the other people I went to high school with were queer. I saw one friend of mine whom I played softball with and soccer with in the gay bar, JR's, one evening. And I've seen her since at things like the AIDS Walk. Her girlfriend plays in my softball league, so I see her just about every week now. We don't really talk about school that much. We just talk about what's going on now. It was never like we went through the formal acknowledgment of each other as queer. It was just like the nodding of, "Yeah, you're queer; I'm queer too." We didn't come out to each other in high school. I hadn't come out at the time she graduated. She graduated when I was a sophomore. I always suspected about her, wondered. And then I saw her in JR's, and it was like, "Aahh!" The light went on.

Mathis

I remember walking down the hall and having people say things and spit on me. I was spit on three times all through my high school life, and I didn't think that happened to anybody else. The first time it happened, somebody spit on my face, right in front of two of my best friends. I didn't do anything about it; I just stood there. And actually, that made him look like an utter fool. Everybody was just looking at him. I never really got in that many fights in high school, amazingly. A lot of straight guys would flirt with me in high school, which was really annoying.

My school was divided halfway down the middle: people who absolutely loved me and people who absolutely hated me. A lot of people by then had gotten to know who I was and liked my character, liked who I was. Other people who didn't know me, didn't want to get to know me, totally hated me. Sometimes they didn't even have to say anything. It wasn't just the way they talked about me; it was the way they sometimes looked at and acted around me. Some people wouldn't even drink from the water fountain after I had been there. Other people would actually say things.

We moved away from Pawnee, to a place called Davenport, where I ended up dropping out of school completely. My mom had told me that I couldn't graduate from Pawnee. In Pawnee, I had been stalked by this particular person, and I had informed teachers and stuff like that. Only one teacher would help me. I told the principal about it. He didn't do anything until the boy came to school with a gun. They found the gun at lunchtime, meaning that the boy had an opportunity to kill me from the time he got to school until lunchtime.

When I moved to Davenport, I started realizing there were certain people at the school who were obsessed with giving me shit. So I dropped out of that high school too and I went to a neighboring town's high school. That was going really good. I had friends there. One person in particular was gay and out, and he was a good friend of mine. And then it started happening again. One particular person just picked me out and was giving me problems, and he found out where I lived. So then I dropped out of high school there, and I never went back. I stayed home in my room for close to two years, didn't do anything.

Michael Talis

I am very lucky to go to the school that I go to. Westtown School is a private, Quaker boarding school almost 200 years old. You are required to board in eleventh and twelfth grades, though most board in the underclassmen years as well. I didn't though because I live so close. The school has incredible morals. It is accepting of any religion, race, sexuality, etc., into its community. The school values each member of the community—the Quaker motto of our school is that there is the "light" or "that of God in all of us." This equality that is based in the Quaker philosophy can really be seen as it plays out at Westtown.

Now it sounds like I'm making a pitch for my school, but it really is the truth. I was pessimistic about this whole communal thing when I heard of Westtown too, but it is the truth. This is my seventh year there, and I've come to admire and respect the Quaker religion and its philosophies. Having my mom Catholic and my dad Jewish, going to a Quaker school was yet another religion that I had to take into consideration. I have adopted Quakerism as my own religion because, it makes more sense in my life than any other religion.

Westtown has no specific policy relating to homosexuals themselves. It will not discriminate on the basis of race, sex, or sexual preference. Westtown does have a specific policy against harassment though. Westtown takes the issue of mutual respect *very* seriously because it is a community. Being a boarding school, it's vital that respect be present, or else people couldn't live together. The school would treat the derogatory comment of "Nigger!" "Fag!" and "Jew!" the same way under the harassment policy. Under most circumstances, you will be expelled if a teacher catches you saying this to someone else, or if the victim repeatedly complains about it. As for the school and homosexual issues, the school is just now joining the 1990s.

As in any other high school, there are many clubs, including the Jewish Students Organization, Student Union for All Persons, Amnesty International, etc. Only about two or three months ago was the Rainbow Alliance started. The Rainbow Alliance is a group that meets regularly to talk about homosexual issues including discrimination, etc. It is led by three teachers, two female and one male, who are all homosexual. They are also working on proposals to the school for setting up a support network for homosexuals, a specific policy relating to homophobia, courses that deal with homosexuals, and more. The group is trying to get the school on top of these issues, and Westtown is very welcoming of it.

The issue of sexuality seems to be coming up more and more at school, so planned for April 17th is a NED on sexuality. A NED is a Nontraditional Educational Day. It's a day where there are no classes, but the whole day is focused on one issue. We have one per trimester, and in the past, they've been about race issues, respect, AIDS, and many other topics. There's a standard format for NED days. There's a keynote speaker in the beginning of the day, the school breaks up into about fifteen to twenty discussion groups and talks about the more specific topic they've all signed up for, lunch, more discussion groups involving some activities of some sort, and at the end of the day, there's a schoolwide event. NEDs are *very* effective in bringing to light an issue that is important to the school as a whole or something that the students are interested in or the faculty think the school should examine more closely. Most students enjoy NEDs because there's no classes; if you set it up right, you can be with your friends the whole day, but you still get a lot out of it. So this upcoming NED on sexuality should be an interesting one.

I just recently came out about being gay to a lesbian teacher at my school. At Westtown, teachers are called either by their first names or by "Teacher so and so." There are no Mr., Mrs., etc. This teacher, Megan, is the only one who knows about me. I felt more comfortable going to her because she was openly lesbian. I knew she *couldn't* reject me! I found it to be one of the most liberating times in my life. Megan was comforting, helpful to talk with, a great source of info about gay issues at Westtown, a great library for info about being homosexual as a teenager, and more. I think that my decision to come out to Megan was one of the best I've ever made.

Mary Toth

I got a lot of teasing from girls about how I looked like a boy. I remember specifically, in fifth grade in Willits, I got a lot of shit for not wearing a bra. I didn't notice that I had breasts. I was a B-cup when I needed a bra in fifth grade, and I just didn't notice. And I didn't wear makeup; I didn't go after boys. The only boy I went after was more my fishing buddy than anything like a boyfriend.

I was excluded from every social circle you could think of. I was a nerd; I was a dyke; I was not happy with my life, so I was an angry little child. So I just sort of separated myself from the crowd in every way, shape, and form.

There was a closeted lesbian group on my high school campus that was mostly made up of basketball players. I got the most shit from them because I came out while I was in high school. I got spat on, and the only people who ever spat on me were other lesbians at my school. So that was kinda weird. It's like the ultimate in antilesbian acceptance. That was kind of trippy, but it was okay because I had my girlfriend at that time.

My junior year of high school, I came out with a shot. I came out in a panel to my high school. I was the little support group dyke at that point. I figured I have support behind me, I can finally do this, and I've always been sort of an activist anyway, and this kind of explained to all the other children why I was always so backwards, I guess. I never got beat up or anything like that. I got called a "dyke." Great. So a bunch of the local good ol' boys would call me "dyke," and I'd turn around and say "Yes?" And they'd sit there and go, "Duh." And I got shouted at.

At some point, I informed one of my best friends that she was a lesbian; she knew herself, and I'd known for a long time. And I was madly in lust with her. I was desperately trying to get down her pants, to put it as crudely as possible. She freaked out. I'd exposed her to every facet of lesbian culture I knew. She'd gotten together with one of the leaders of the in-the-closet lesbian group and rejected me because I was out. So I had a lot of stuff going on with that. Then a year later, she called me up and thanked me for bringing her out.

Paige

A couple of kids at my high school got suspended because they had a sticker on their car that read, "Stop AIDS, Stop Fags." They were kicked out for a week, I think—maybe three days or something. But their suspension by my principal was definitely the result of pressure from a very progressive teacher in my high school. Earlier, my principal actually had to go through sensitivity training for a comment he made at a Los Gatos Lions Club speech. He said that the Golden Gate Bridge connected jungleland and fairyland. I don't know the whole joke, but it was pretty bad. He also said other things about how women shouldn't jog because they'll bruise their eyes. So sensitivity wasn't really a strong point for him.

There are no out teachers at Los Gatos High. I know of one queer person there, but she's still not out. She's still there, though. I know of one other person who's also queer, and she's definitely not out and definitely not going to be anytime soon. Unfortunately, she will never do it because I think there's probably a good chance that she would either be demoted or somehow lose her job. I think it's completely appropriate for a teacher to be out at school. I think it lends a support network to some of the kids who might look for someone to talk to. Although, I think it's the teacher's personal decision.

I think a lesbian would definitely be more accepted by the students than a gay man being an out teacher. I think, in general, that's pretty true. In my town, it seems to be. I'm sure there'd be the normal little fly of rumors around and about, and a couple of people, a couple of the jocks going "dyke, dyke," and shit like that. But really, aside from the consequences of the administration who might feel they're doing the best things for the kids if they fire the teacher, I think the student body would be pretty okay about it. I'm sure there'd be a lot under their breath. Apathy perhaps.

It was almost summer, right before school had ended, so I was still fifteen. I went to lunch with four of my close friends and I just put it out on the table that I was bi—here it is. That's how I've learned to live my life, I think. Anyhow, three of them were supportive, and one was like, "Oh, okay, that's cool," that type of thing. About a week later, I think the whole school knew. I don't know for sure, but I know it had definitely been passed along the grapevine.

Then my scooter was banged up. It was bent up and "dyke" was written on the side of it. I quit that day. I'd had a lot of troubles and personal problems before that. I didn't like high school. That was just the icing on the cake. I just felt like shit; I cried. I don't think there's any other way to describe it; I felt almost violated. That might be a strong term, considering the guy who did it never came anywhere near me. I knew who did it though. He obviously didn't even have the balls to face me. The guy's just an asshole. It's not even worth dealing with 'cause he's such a dick.

I did bring it to the attention of the vice principal. She said, "It's just graffiti; it doesn't mean anything; it wasn't directed at anyone special. I'm sure it wasn't directed at you." And just wrote it off as graffiti, and school security took a picture of it and said they'd try to find out who did it.

At that time in high school, I was tired of everyone, and I knew that I was beyond that. Those four girls who were my friends in high school were about the only four people I ever talked to on a regular basis. I had a lot of older friends who went to DeAnza College, and I spent a lot of time with them. I realized high school was not for me. When you can't tell someone in confidence something like that and the whole school knows, I don't know. It had just been building up the last semester. Little things, like teachers who were just really rude to me. I had a biology teacher who told our whole class that we would be nothing. That was one of the reasons I dropped out. He made that whole year a living hell for me. Just recently, I went down to my old high school and I showed them my report card because I got a 3.7 on my first set of college grades. Oh, I felt so good! Dropping out of high school was the best thing I ever did.

Todd Fay-Long

When I moved to a new junior high, and I made a lot of new friends, I got in with a new crowd. I still wasn't into the whole popular thing, though. Junior high was the worst. My theory is that no one wants attention drawn to them, and no one wants anyone to notice that they're different, so they point at other people. Junior high pretty much just sucked, but I finally got through it. Then I went to high school in Petaluma. I started at a school called Casa Grande. I was going there, doing a lot of drugs, and I was just partying and getting into trouble.

Now I feel like I wanted or preferred for people to think of me as a druggie than to think of me as being gay. I felt that way at that point, but I don't feel that way now. So I was getting in trouble a lot; I got really drunk one time and the cops came and had my mom come get me. A couple weeks later, I got busted for drug paraphernalia at school. So the cops called my mom again, and she had to come get me.

I was still pretty much doing drugs and stuff like that, and I OD'd one time, and I had to go to the hospital. That was really a turning point for me because, first, it made me realize that I needed to get my shit together. And second, it made me realize that I needed to find ways to be happy. I was just really unhappy at the school I was going to. I was getting bad grades, and school just seemed like a jail. I transferred and I started going to this private continuation school. It was really cool. You learned if you wanted to, and you were really more in charge of your education and what you were learning. I still wasn't out, though. At that school, you didn't really graduate. You just took your proficiency test, your GED, and then you're done. That was just a better environment for me.

I'm comfortable with being gay, and I like to go to gay clubs, but I just think I wouldn't have been able to do this if I was still in high school. I would be a much different person, and I probably wouldn't be out. One of the high schools I went to has a United Sexualities Club now, which it didn't have when I was there. I think the club's really good because it just increases visibility on the campus. Actually, the teacher who runs that club now was my English teacher when I was there. He's gay, and he would wear his pride T-shirts to school and stuff like that. He was really a role model. I thought I wanted to teach for a while because of him.

Jim

My school's really cliquey. When you walk down in the quad area, there's these groups of people gathering, and they're just gossiping, and there's a lot of whispering. I usually have my headphones on, listening to music. I don't really worry about it; I just go to class and go to my next class.

I'm a person who goes to school to learn, not to socialize. I see friends there and I see people I know, but it's just like going to work. You get your business done and then you leave. And if somebody happens to call me a fag or whatever they want to call me, I don't let it get to me. I just say, "Fuck you."

Chapter 7

CyberQueer: Finding Community on the Internet

Adam Hardy

I've discovered a strange sort of gay community on the Internet. This was how I met my friend Jeremy (through #gayteen on IRC), another guy named Nick, and several other people who are in my life right now. The USENET newsgroup soc.support.youth.gay-lesbian-bi (ssyglb) is another very good example of this, and I've made six or seven friends this way.

Coming out then was probably the best thing I've done in my life, and I gained more self-confidence and strength then than I think I ever had in my life. I went from being repressed to confident, outgoing, and at times outrageous.

This was good because I was then dealing with the one thing they *don't* tell you about—loneliness. I guess a lot of gay teenagers must miraculously find one another, but I never really did.

Connecting with the "queer community" has always been a strange thing for me. When I came out to my mother, she wanted to join PFLAG, but we found out that the local chapter had been disbanded due to "lack of interest." Our national coming-out day was nineteen people getting harassed in the park. We only recently got our first gay bookstore. There's nothing to be found in the phone book, and there was no information available in my high school. I didn't feel safe with the counselors there anyway—my instinct was that they'd be homophobic, and I've had little reason to believe otherwise. I've met a guy at home via ssyglb who wants to put together a gay youth group in my hometown, and I intend to help him do so.

Alan Wiley

The first time I told someone that I might be gay I was thirteen- or fourteen-years-old, probably closer to fourteen. It was my freshman year in high school, and I was on Prodigy, the computer service, and I met a guy, and he just started talking to me, and the subject got to being gay, and I told him that I thought I might be gay. And he told me that he was seventeen years old, and so I felt like I could relate to him. And I wrote to him all the time, and we always talked.

Later on, he told me that he was thirty-three, and I was upset, 'cause we had gotten to be good friends, and that bothered me that he lied to me. That was my first experience talking to another person whom I knew to be gay. At that point, I told him I was bisexual because I thought it would be better to be bisexual than to be totally gay.

A few months after that, I had the same kind of experience. I was out to a few more people then, but I met another thirty-three-year-old guy on the computer, who subsequently fell in love with me. And it was, not really an emotionally scarring experience, but it was kind of a scarring experience, because I had two thirty-three-year-old men that were in love with me. I'm thirteen or fourteen, seriously questioning my sexuality; they were nice people; I'm glad nothing ever happened, and, I don't know, it just reaffirmed my belief that I needed to stick to who I was and not try to be something that other people wanted me to be.

Ernie Hsiung

As far as meeting other gay folks are concerned, I meet other people through the Internet.

Michael Talis

I have been thinking about classifying myself as "gay" for a long time. I have known that I'm more attracted to men for about a year or two. It's only been within the last six months or so that I've come to the realization that I am definitely gay and need to do something about it. This "doing something" includes either discussing it with someone, seeking out a gay realtionship, and/or getting involved with gay-related issues and groups. I spend a lot of time thinking about the issue of being gay, where I'll be later in life because of it, how I can deal with it now, friends'/family reactions, and more. Coming to the realization that I am definitely gay has been my first big step.

The voices inside my head saying, "Mike, you're gay; now take the next step," have been getting stronger the more I discuss gay issues and my sexuality. The Internet newsgroup soc.support.youth.gay-lesbian-bi is what finally convinced me to come out and tell someone—this was only four days before this interview.

Paige

A friend of mine, Nathan, who went to Simon's Rock, had been pulled out of Simon's Rock in second semester because he had just started dating another guy there; Nathan's gay, and his parents found some letters supporting this. His parents are extreme religion people, and he was pulled out of Simon's Rock two days before it was supposed to start again and put into an extremely religious school in Illinois. So I've been on-line a lot with him, researching groups on-line, because he couldn't get it though his on-line service; it was blocked. So I'd be sending him the mail about stuff, just kind of helping him out. He definitely needs help, and the only way we can communicate is through e-mail.

Chapter 8

Community Views: The Lesbian/Bi/Gay World and Beyond

FINDING PEERS/FINDING COMMUNITY

The move from personal questioning to connection with a visible community cannot be understated in terms of its significance as a highly charged political statement. It is notable that many of the youth who participated in this project found stability and an outlet for their political desires for queer-friendly social spaces through connection with a broader queer community. Although there are obvious social motivations—increasingly so, as the amount of youth community participation grows—the outcome has been a radical reenergizing of the queer political movement. With this push, however, comes a degree of pressure that rests heavily on the minds and backs of youth doing queer political work.

Chapters 8 and 9 explore both initial impressions of, and involvement in, the queer community. Several of the youth in this collection recount their first encounters with someone queer. The validation they experienced meeting someone else like them is profound. Equally profound, though, is the amount of fear and trepidation they felt as they came across images of adult queers in their search for others similar to themselves. Before meeting other queer people, many of the youth held the common, horrific, societal stereotypes of queers. Finding adults from various walks of life with a range of experiences and backgrounds placed queerness in a context of normalcy that just did not fit with those negative images they had been fed.

Many of the young people in this collection speak of the overwhelmingly positive experience of eventually meeting other queer youth through youth groups connected to youth service agencies.

Meeting others who can relate so closely to one's own experiences takes validation to an entirely different level. And the solidarity of fighting for similar changes in an oppressive system leads to an incredibly strong front for political action. Having suffered alone, and perhaps been the only out person in their schools or communities, these young people see and use the strength to be found in their numbers when they stand united as youth.

Ironically, however, the potential for political burnout is high among these youth. Their drive to make change happen for themselves as well as their peers means they often take on the burden of representing other youth less comfortable with being publicly out (not to mention the queer community at large).

Unique to this generation is a pride in, and an embracing of, who they are, accelerated by the growing acceptance (or at least awareness) of queer sexuality as compared to attitudes from only a decade before. This growth has meant the opportunity to spend far less time in an agonizing closet of shame, allowing these young people to find validation and support in others like themselves (if they are lucky enough to live near or in a large city with services or have a connection to the Internet) and personally develop and grow in their queer identities from relatively early ages. With this pride, they are better equipped than a number of their adult peers to fight for their place at society's table.

In short, queer youth often have the stability and security in identity to fight publicly for their rights to be respected and represented in society. It is unfortunate that, more often than not, they do not receive support from either the straight or queer community; they end up taking on the lion's share of battles facing their communities. But, as the stories related in this chapter attest, they are working with the resources available to them and affecting incredible amounts of change in the process.

* * *

Anthony Gomez

The first time I did anything gay was going to the Castro. I just loved it. I could be a flame all I wanted to, and nobody sat there going, "Omigod! What a fucking queer!" or something like that.

I just thought that was really cool. That's what I loved about it. I went there with friends. I came out to one of my friends. I said, "I think I'm gay." And he was like, "Whoa, let's go to Castro and we'll see if you're gay. We'll do a test there." And I said, "Okay, test me, Baby!" And so we went out. The second place I went to was a bar called JR's. I didn't order anything; I just wanted to go in there and see what the gay scene was all about. I liked it a lot. I saw this cute guy who was really cool.

I saw that you could be who you want to be. When I came out to my mom, I said, "Mom, I'm gay—don't hit me!" But I found out I can be who I am; I can be a queen! I finally found a place where I'm not the black sheep anymore. It was cool finding a place I belonged.

Adam Hardy

I came out here at my school, Simon's Rock, after about three days. By "came out," I mean that as part of a class discussion I gathered up my courage and mentioned in a conversation that I was gay.

From that moment on, I was publicly out on campus. I also met the first noncloseted gay man I'd ever met in my life, who went by the name of San Trask. He was a Goth type, meaning he looked scary, but he was actually quiet, shy, and friendly. He was living with his boyfriend on campus, and they were *quite* out. What I'd heard about the school was true—there really isn't any overt homophobia here.

Up until this point, I'd never experienced much of a "gay community." Simon's Rock was strange that way—because of our size, we really didn't have many gay people to form a community. Nevertheless, my school's BiGaLA meetings and our Queer Film Festival were my first exposure to the gay community, seeing movies such as *Tales of the City, Maurice, The Lost Language of Cranes, Torch Song Trilogy,* and *Longtime Companion.*

My first connection to a gay community in Huntsville came when two passersby noticed a pair of freedom rings I was wearing, sent by my friend Nick in Massachusetts, and I met Rebekah and Troll. Rebekah and I went to the local Metropolitan Community Church and discovered the existence of Rainbow's Ltd., the local bookstore. I found out about the new local club, the Upscale; though, being eighteen, I can't get in, but I still have no strong connections.

My theory is still that most well-adjusted gay people have long since evacuated my hometown of Huntsville.

Eileene Coscolluela

I used to be *very* homophobic. I used to use the Bible to speak against homosexual acts. I was terrible. I thought that the glbt community was just a bunch of perverts, especially seeing and hearing about nothing but their sexual promiscuity. As I began to know the community better, I learned that this was not the case. I learned that there were people who had the same relationship for years. We're "normal" people. The stereotypes aren't the rule; they are the exception.

I feel that the gay community must make this clear in order to be accepted. I feel like the community is tearing itself apart because of this. I feel a very strong connection to the glbt community.

Dawn McCausland

A panel from a support group called Positive Images came to my peer support class in high school. That was the first time that I had ever seen a gay youth. I didn't know anyone who had an active gay lifestyle under forty years old, except my hairdresser—really stereotypic stuff like that.

I'd never had older gay role models, older gay people in my life. I didn't know any teachers, school administrators, students; there weren't even rumors about it. That's how isolated it was. At this time, I was living out on the beach in Bodega Bay, and then also in Forestville, which is a small town right next to Guerneville, both in northern California.

Guerneville has a lot of gay people, but there's tension with the rest of the community. There weren't that many children of gay people, and there was a lot of homophobia with the rest of the community. Everybody made jokes about Guerneville. My high school was pretty homophobic.

I remember the first time I ever saw a flier for a gay youth support group. My friend, the girl that I had a crush on, and I were walking around school, and I just remember she found it on the ground, and we were like, "A group like this exists?!" and "This is at our high school?" I was sixteen years old then, and that was so amazing to me, to have any contact with someone who was gay.

So I started to come out. I saw a queer youth speakers' panel. It blew me away, but I didn't self-define that way. It took me three months and three hang-up calls to actually call the organization that sponsored the panel presentations and say that I wanted to be in the support group. It was really hard for me to do that. I didn't really have any support. I wasn't really telling anyone. I was dropping hints to my family, talking about the panel, or talking about this and that. But I was so freaked out.

I also remember doing a lot of interesting journal writings. I would clip out—not necessarily pictures of people, because I didn't know any gay stars, so to say—but any article that possibly had to do with gay people, in any newspaper or magazine that I got hold of. It was around the time of the March on Washington, and *Newsweek* was coming out with cover stories on the military ban—it was everywhere. I remember being really enthralled by it, like, "Those are what they look like," just staring at the pictures.

But then, accompanying every positive picture, there was also a negative picture of some homophobic person saying, "God hates faggots," or whatever it was. That freaked me out. It was, "Okay, yes, people are alive and I can be like this and I can live a happy life." And then it was also, "I'm gonna have to fight forever to be able to be this way." So it was a scary time.

It wasn't until I started doing activism that I ever met anyone who was older, out, and gay. Basically, until I came out, the only gay people I knew about were closeted gay people and young people. Even my hairdresser, whom I went to for six years was still very, very boundaried about it, and wouldn't really talk about it—talked around it a lot, implied it—but wouldn't really talk about it. It was honestly a pretty negative thing. Because it was like, "Why aren't you talking about it? I know about it; you know about it. Why the silence? What's wrong with it?" That's part of what gave me an idea that it really is something wrong, and it really is something that you can't talk to other people about. I wasn't used to that. I'm used to talking about major parts of my life and my feelings.

One of my strongest first impressions of older gay people was when I started to take junior college classes and I could pick out older gay people in my classes, especially the lesbians I saw there. I mean, I have gaydar. Here I was in my gung ho coming-out stage, everything was gay, everything was pride, pride, pride. Every conversation, every classroom. I had just been out a couple of months, but I would be doing speeches on it in my speech class, or whatever. And then after class, I would have older gay people pull me aside in secluded areas and tell me, "Oh, well, I'm one of you," or "Yeah, I know what you mean; I'm like that too." A lot of times they wouldn't even say it. They wouldn't come up to me and say, "Hi, I'm a lesbian, nice to meet you." They were just like, "Yeah, well, I'm like that too." It was really almost an insult. I think I would have rather not known. I am a "baby" dyke; I've only been out a couple months; I have no security behind me and these women weren't helping me.

It was like I was being stuck on the front lines; it's my job to take care of my own identity, but to be the one who's taking all the heat in the class, even when I bring it up, for them not to discuss it in a classroom discussion is really disappointing to me. And so, aside from a couple of the activist older gay people I worked with, I had a very bad image of older gay people; they were all closeted, and they weren't okay about it. I was writing a paper once with a lesbian—it was a group paper—and two straight women who are very open-minded about it. The topic was a comparison of punk culture and the gay culture in Sonoma County. This woman would still refer to basically her wife as her roommate every single time we talked. It was, "Hello, hi, we're writing a paper on gay people, and we know you're gay. You don't need to talk about your wife as your roommate." It was really disappointing, and it gave me such a bad image of my future and about what the possibilities were. It was like there was something wrong with me for being that out. I really didn't understand that. So those were some of my first impressions.

Now I know more older gay people, and I understand where they're coming from more; I understand what they've been through and the persecution they went through compared to me. Here it is, the Gay '90s. Things aren't great, but they're a lot better. I'm not coming from all the shit that they got. I understand that more now. I still do get frustrated with the older gay community. I don't interact that much with them because I don't find enough people who incorporate being gay into their lives; being gay is kind of separate, and they just don't involve themselves that much.

Eriq Chang

I have a lot of gay friends. I mostly hang out with people outside of high school because I really don't like a lot of people in high school. I socialize a lot, but the people I mostly hang out with are college-type and just have all types of sexuality. I have friends who are gay, trans, just a whole bunch of different types of people.

I feel more open with gay kids than with other kids. I feel more comfortable, and it sounds corny and hokey and stupid, but I feel more brotherly. I feel like we know each other. I know several gay adults. I guess I just think of the person. I really don't know too many people who are around or under my age who are gay, bisexual, or lesbian. But I do know several people in college.

The gay community's a little too raucous for me! I saw my first gay magazine at Tower Records. It was pretty much pornographic. I was like, "Oh, hot, baby." My first impression was, "Omigod, the whole gay industry is all about sex." The gay community is very sexual; well, I would have to say as sexual as the straights. They're very aimed at the entertainment and the looks-type feel. Especially gay men.

I went to Castro and thought, "This is so fucking trendy." Everyone has shaved heads and short hair and they're really butch looking and they have leather or else, and that was my impression. Just like there was no real relationship out there. I'm being totally honest. That's what I got. Now I know better than that. I know people who are gay and people who are bi, and they have relationships and they're totally content. They're just people. I don't call it a lifestyle either. I hate it when people say, "Oh, the bisexual and the lesbian and the gay lifestyle." It's not a lifestyle; it's a life. We're people. We shouldn't be labeled.

It felt strange at first. I saw these two guys totally like, "Oh, hi, honey, I haven't seen you in the longest time," and they pecked on the cheek. I thought, "Whoa!" because that's something I've wanted to do, not just in Castro, but in public. I see people holding hands, and it's something that I want.

When I was in the Castro, I just got the impression that everyone there knows who they are. Now I don't really think the Castro is that big of a deal. I think of it as sort of another club. When I go there, I feel like it's not just a gay street; it's almost a tourist attraction.

Lisa Campbell

I didn't know too much about the community before I started trying to come out. When I moved out of my dad's house in the end of May, beginning of June, it was under bad circumstances. I stayed at my ex's for a few days. And then my friend Shalyn, who's mother is a lesbian and lives with her partner, said, "Hey, my family have all talked about it, and we all agree that you should come and live with us for a while until you get on your feet." So that's what I did. And I stayed there a few months. It was good that there was someone watching over me. Part of the reason they were willing to do that for so long was because I was gay and so were they.

Mathis

My uncle is gay. I hadn't met him till I was probably fifteen. Everybody called him Aunt Roy and stuff like that. I totally, totally hate the man. He is very, very annoying; he tells people that he has sex with animals and stuff like that. I kept telling everyone, "He is not gay," but he never hid being gay. He always had gay paraphernalia around his house, in front of my family. So it was rather hard for me to come out. In some ways, I consider him a bad role model, and in some ways not.

He was very out, but he gave my family a bad impression of what gay people are like. I kept looking for a good gay role model whom I could refer to. I couldn't find that many. Now it's very easy because a lot of people are open and out and everything. I think it's really unusual, the amount of people who are in music and television who are gay, because everybody says there aren't that many.

I guess the only exposure to the gay community that I had was a magazine, *The Advocate,* that my uncle and I would read. I would see that and know that there was a place I could go and that I had to get away. And then whenever I came here to Santa Rosa, I actually started meeting people.

I knew about Parents and Friends of Lesbians and Gays—PFLAG—before, but it didn't interest me because that's not my mother's type of thing, and it's not my aunt and uncle's type of thing because they don't have time. But through that, I learned about the insides of PFLAG and then joined a local youth group, Positive Images.

To me, it's meant friendship; I mean true friendship. It's quite unusual because, as soon as I went there, people were embracing me; that was really nice. PFLAG is a parents organization. A PFLAG member cofounded our group, Positive Images. PFLAG is not important in my life, but I know for other people it is because their parents are members; it's just a really good support group. I've met some of the members of PFLAG and realized how it helped them deal with their homophobia toward their children. I have no idea what it would be like to be homophobic toward your own children.

Project Ten is another group I found out about that has gay-friendly or gay members of high schools who are all part of Project Ten within the high schools; they're just people who youth can go to, talk to about their sexuality, their feelings, things like that. They have problems with being accused of recruiting.

To me, all these groups make me feel like . . . it's just home. They're full of support for me, endless support. You could just meet a gay person on the street, and you already have something in common with him; I feel a bond, like a family bond. I use the term family whenever I talk to other gay people, and we ask each other, "Well, are they family?" I was worried that once I move away from my aunt and uncle, then I'll have no family. And then I was lying in bed the other night and realized that's utter bullshit. I have family. Just because they're not related to me bloodwise doesn't mean they're not family.

Michael Talis

My first encounter with the glbt community was at the AIDS Walk I did this spring in Philadelphia. Before we went to the walk, the group from my school that went to the walk went to the Philadelphia Monthly Meeting—just a bigger Meeting for Worship. At this meeting, I heard many stories about how AIDS is affecting the gay community. Artists, teachers, and the average tax-paying American stood up and told their side of it. I was really moved by what many of them had to say. I had several realizations at this Meeting.

The first thing I did when the person stood up and said they were gay was compare them with the gay man/woman's stereotype. And, to my surprise, not many fit the stereotype. Most of the people who stood up and said something were also HIV positive/had AIDS. Seeing that there were a bunch of people who stood up, I realized that AIDS is something real that I have to be worried about.

Considering that I'm not openly gay, except to one person, I'm not as connected to the glbt community as I could/should be. I do feel a connection to my lesbian teacher who knows about my sexuality. We've talked on several occasions about my feelings, what I should do, and her experiences being an open lesbian. I've found talking very helpful, and we've grown much closer because of it.

Mary Toth

When I ran away from home, I had to estrange myself from everybody, including my support group, because I didn't want to feel responsible for my parents, who kinda went insane looking for me and started calling up everybody, including the facilitator of my support group. One of my main role models in the queer community at that point had been my friend Donna, who's pretty much my lesbian mom. My God! This woman saved me when I was at home. She was one of my major role models. She lived a block away from me in Healdsburg, and her kids were the same age I was. She showed me what it's like to be an autonomous woman—a lesbian—raising two children on her own, who never had a husband, had various girlfriends, and had established herself. She's an electrician, and she has everything together. She has financial stability; she's a good mom, all these sorts of things.

When I ran away, I extricated myself from the gay and lesbian community that I'd previously been a part of, doing panel discussions, doing support group work, things like that. I basically had to force myself into isolation because the sheriff's department was coming by trying to find me, and my parents were trying to look for me, and they wanted to haul me back home. I was seventeen at this time.

I had previously been in the queer community as sort of an active participant. I felt like I owed the community something because they'd allowed me a community in general, which I hadn't had up until that point. And they'd also showed me about interpersonal relationships and personal growth and things like that. But being in that isolation was really strange for me, while I was in hiding, and that's when I started exposing myself to more of the Castro side of things. I figured

I was safe from my parents because who's gonna find me in the Castro? So I went to the Castro, and I hung out a lot at Café San Marcos—a bar in the Castro.

It was mostly a girl bar then. There was a very cliquey feel to it sometimes. There were a lot of folks from all types of backgrounds. It was kinda nice, though, because at the San Marcos they didn't wig out because I was desperately poor. I got to know the bartenders. I'd hang out there for hours, sometimes for an entire day. I'd just sit up there and read or draw or something like that while my girlfriend was off stripping and making money for the house. They wouldn't balk at me if I only got a glass of water and stuff like that. And they could tell I needed a place to hang out—I was desperately thin; I looked bad at that time. I was down to about 135 pounds, and I'm six foot and a half, so that was not good. Especially considering I was 188 pounds when I left home.

I got a lot of people picking up on me. It was kind of funny. I found out that books are a great intro; people will come up and ask you what you're reading. So I got to see a lot of the more social, older aspects of the dyke community, which was kinda neat because I'd always had a sense of that, but I'd never been an active participant in the older bar scene. And I realized that I'd always sort of wanted to experience that; I'd read about that older bar scene and I wanted to be just like that when I grew up. I wanted to be like the rad player dyke from Hell—somebody who fucks around just so they can, someone who works the scene and doesn't particularly care who she's screwing, no emotional attachment. Of course, I'm incapable of being a player; I have the problem that I wind up falling in love with anybody I sleep with, so that kinda cuts me out of the spectrum.

Later, I moved back to Santa Rosa, which was nice 'cause it was more centrally located, and I could get more involved in the queer community. I sort of considered myself a "freelance dyke" after I had to isolate myself from everything. But I'd formed more of a lesbian community with my girlfriend, 'cause she had a lot of older dyke friends who'd go out dancing on a regular basis. So I'd go dancing at Aunt Ruby's, which is a little club in San Rafael, and I established some pretty good friendships there. I have older dyke friends who are forty-six and others in their twenties to forties to late forties. It was very family oriented. It was almost like I had a bunch of lesbian moms. And that was very new—but it wasn't political, and it wasn't socially outreaching, it was an impromptu gathering of women that I found a lot of ties through. It was more a loving community.

I had a problem, though, with some of the older lesbians because they seemed to almost be acting out the new social scenes, like the player sort of stereotype. Hitting on each other and trying to play the scene and things like that. Being very social about it, and not getting into the more political aspects of the lesbian community. Although I'm not an active member, it's very true to my beliefs that one should feel responsible for your community and feel responsible about upholding some of the politics of that community. They were more like playing a role. They were political in their own way—they were more into the goddess worship scene and reclaiming the ritual and such; I can totally understand that from their perspective. Most of these folks were raised in strictly religious families and things like that. But for me, I was more interested in the politics—what can we do now, how can we change things now. I'm sort of a radical girl anyway, as it were; I'm always into a fight of the system. I just didn't feel a lot of that coming from the older lesbians. So I felt kind of estranged from that.

I started working the social scene after I broke up with my third girlfriend. For the past six months, I've basically been a slut. I have been serially monogamous—I'm not sure if you could really call it that, because it never lasted long enough to be called monogamy. But I started exploring more social aspects of the gay and lesbian community, not really having time to engage in any of the political aspects or anything like that. I didn't have time to join an organization, because I've been working continuously and supporting myself since I left home, and that can be a very difficult thing when you're not getting paid a lot. I went back to school, so I didn't have as many hours available for activist work. I went back to Santa Rosa Junior College, and I'm currently working to transfer out.

My overall impression of the community is that it's actually very segmented in Sonoma County. There are the youth activist folks; there are the older sort of more ritual-oriented lesbians, the activist dykes, the nerd dykes, the Queer dykes, and of course, baby dykes, who are people just coming out. Then there's the sort of midrange of folks who aren't really belonging to any sort of activity, but they just sort of hang out. There is a community there, but we don't really come together as a single unified community a lot. There's not one cohesive group. There's no sense of community. Maybe that's just because I don't live in the city, but I'd like to get more involved in that. I feel like there is more unity down here.

Paige

My sister had one lesbian friend, whom I'm now really good friends with, and my dad's secretary was gay; that was all the exposure I ever had to the gay community in my town. But as I went on in age and discovered, "Hey, this is what I'm looking for," I sought it out. I sought out the Billy deFrank Center in San Jose, and other types of support.

When I talk with older lesbians and gay men, they're definitely shocked. When they were sixteen, being out was definitely not an option. My good friend Kate is I think twenty-seven, something like that. Ten years ago, in the mid-1980s, she told me there was no way she would ever come out at sixteen. She told me, "My parents would have shipped me off to some psychotherapist and gotten me help." She didn't come out until after her first marriage. So she definitely lived a way different lifestyle than I did.

I definitely see different sexual identities, but I think, at least in Massachusetts, where most of my community is, it mixes very well. I realize the difference in every person, but I don't see them as the lesbian community, the gay community, the bisexual community, and so on, and so on, and so on.

When you walk through Northampton, you see that everyone is there and together. Like the Hay Market, a place I like to hang out, is not just a dyke bar. It's a bar that almost everyone in Northampton goes to. Straight, gay, purple, green, yellow, whatever. But, for me, it represents a really great time. And I think there's definitely a whole community there. It's not so separated. I see San Francisco and the Bay area as a little bit more separated than Northampton. I don't know. But maybe since I grew up here, I have a different view of it. But I definitely see more of the lines on the West Coast in general. I've been in LA and to Northampton and also to the gay district in Boston, and it's much more mixed. There aren't as many lines, I don't think.

Todd Fay-Long

The first club I went to was JR's. The first time I went there, I got really drunk, and I got together with this guy; we were totally making out, and I almost went home with him. But my friend Jeff grabbed my hand and said, "Think about it." It turned out that the guy Jeff kept me from leaving with wanted me to get with him and his boyfriend at the same time, so I'm glad I didn't go. Some intro to the gay community!

I have a fake ID, so I can go to clubs, but I like to go to places that are all ages. I really prefer to go to dance parties. Places that are all ages are good because then I can meet people my age. And I like to go to places that are mixed, like gay and straight, because it seems like when I go to gay places, I get stares just because I'm young and a lot of guys just want to get with younger guys. And I don't respect that.

Jim

I only know one person who's gay and out. We've been friends since the fourth grade. He's cool. Pleasanton's this big bubble, and everybody's just heterosexual, Republican, and tight ass. I'm really sick of it. In a few years, I'm gonna go to San Francisco State. There's no diversity in Pleasanton at all, so it really just conforms. Sometimes I find myself conforming just to get by. It's pretty sad. I don't belong there; I just know I don't belong there.

My first encounter with the queer community was the Castro. Definitely. A friend took me down to Castro, and I was just totally stupid to the whole thing. We went, and he bought some shirts like, "Nobody knows I'm a drag queen." And I got the "Recovering Catholic" shirt.

I think people in the Castro are a lot more open, and they really know how to have fun. If you're gay, bisexual, whatever, it's what you want to do. The whole point in life is to have fun and enjoy life. So if you're gonna enjoy life, I think that's just great.

I have a teacher at school who's gay, and he hasn't told anybody. He's really secretive about it, and I and my closest friend are the only ones who know at school. This teacher and I became friends. He's a really nice person. Everybody likes him. But I'm sure if people found out about it, they'd just totally back off from him. There's no sort of gay community at my school that would be supportive.

Chapter 9

Getting Involved: Extracurriculars in the Community

Anthony Gomez

I'm in a speakers bureau. We talk about how sympathy or empathy from teachers and counselors of high schools is important. The teachers ask questions; we answer questions. We try to help as much as possible. I hope the teachers listen to us. Some don't and some do.

I have a gay therapist. He's really cool. I go to a group; it's in Hayward. You get stressed out, you talk a lot, and that's cool. I like it. I go out—sometimes with the group, and we'll go to the Castro and we'll hang out and that's real cool. I have friends who are gay. Most of the friends I take out are either accepting of me being gay or they are gay.

Alan Wiley

I went to one gay support group—actually I'm lying; I went to two gay support groups. I went to a Gay Youth Alliance in San Diego; that was the first gay youth group I went to. I almost shit in my pants before I went, I was so scared. I had just recently come out to a couple of my friends, and I went with a friend of mine who knew my friends, who had come out to them as being bisexual. She brought me to Gay Youth Alliance for the first time.

I was so afraid. I walked into this room, and there were about forty people just sitting around. It was so strange to think that these people were all gay. It was really, really scary. And we just talked about issues. It was more of a place to meet people, I think, than to really settle issues with yourself.

I was in another gay support group at my high school. After I came out in high school, my boyfriend at the time, who was a sophomore, came out about a week after I did. And that's when people just started coming out. Other kids started coming out to us, and we would basically just meet every once in a while and discuss things. We all knew one another were gay, but no one really outside of that circle knew what was going on. We would just meet at lunchtime sometimes and talk about what was going with us and how we were doing, and keep each other in check, making sure that we were all okay with who we were. We also would plan on going out together and stuff. I think that support was more beneficial to me because it kept me going, while the original support got me to come out.

Eileene Coscolluela

We have a small youth organization in town called GALES, but they aren't very active (unfortunately). Back home in New Jersey, there is GALYNJ and BiGLYNY, but I wasn't active in any of the three organizations.

My best friend here is gay, and we have a wonderful relationship. The local campus organization of lesbian, gays, bisexuals, and transgendered individuals is very small. There are about ten to twenty to thirty truly active people in the association. The glbt community here is not very politically active. They tend to isolate themselves from the rest of campus, and that just causes more distress than help. It makes glbt individuals look unapproachable and segregated, and I don't care too much for that. I wish they would be more *out* and involved.

I wish the professors and teachers who are gay would be more out and more gay people on campus would get involved with the *politics* rather than just the social life of the campus. That kind of upsets me, but that's just the way they deal with their sexuality.

Everything that this campus has dealing with glbt issues, I attend. I might not be an active participant, but just being counted at rallies (I went to Stonewall as well) is what is important.

I feel a different connection with the glbt community than with the straight community because I think that we've all been through the same feelings and the same coming-out process. I have a bisexual female friend (she's pretty closeted), and when we were at the AIDS quilt showing on campus, she came up to me and gave me a big hug without speaking. We've both lost friends in the gay community to AIDS, and it was just a strong, powerful feeling. I talked about it to my boyfriend (a heterosexual male), and he couldn't really understand the powerfulness of the event and how emotional she and I became about the situation.

Dawn McCausland

Meeting young gay people was really profound for me. That's the only word that I can say fits. It changed me a lot, gave me a lot of strength. I started to realize that my sense of reality was fucked, and that people weren't going to hate me—that some people were, but not everybody. I felt like being gay would invalidate everything that I had worked for and everything that I was, and that if anybody found out, then everything, all the work that I had done, would just be useless, and I would be a horrible person, despite everything else that was good about me. I started to realize that the culture was telling me that, and that the people in my life weren't telling me that at all.

Eriq Chang

I haven't really done too much as far as getting involved in the community though. I really wanted to go to the Halloween Castro party thing. I really wanted to perform or something. I've been to several clubs; I've been to Universal and Club X in San Francisco and I went to the AIDS Dance-a-Thon.

Since I live so far away in Pleasanton, I don't go to too many places. I've been to the gay bar, JR's, and I have snuck in. I walked in there, and I was like, "Oh, whoa." I've been to very, very few places where all men or all women hang out. I really just like to go to clubs in general. My first impression of JR's was that it was hot and I was sweating, and I wanted to take off all my clothes and go, "Omigod, take me!" It was fun; it was a lot of fun. I love dancing.

There are no gay support clubs at my school. Nothing at all. I think a club would be difficult to have in Pleasanton, and at the school that I go to, I think it would be totally a heated subject, and all the jocks would go hang out there and see who shows up so they know who's gay. That's the type of society it is over there.

I don't live in the city, but I know there's a lot of gay support groups there, but I don't go to any. Usually, I don't meet people who are my age who are gay or bi. I think a group in Pleasanton would be a good thing though. Yes, I do. I sort of have come to that for me, myself, personally—I don't feel like I really need to go to youth groups and stuff anymore—maybe to help other people.

Ernie Hsiung

The first time I went to a gay youth "support" group was when I was fifteen. I went to a group in Berkeley. I guess I was expecting there to be people like me. There weren't. Instead they were cliquish and arrogant. The only people they would talk to were people who acted/looked like them, and since I wasn't like them, I didn't belong in their little group. I ended up never going to a group again, and to this day, going to a support group makes me uncomfortable. Currently, I meet other people through the Internet.

Kyallee Santanders

My first night at a gay youth group was an awkward one, but the other kids were just like me—not the weirdos society said they'd be—and I could easily identify with what they felt and what they were going through. I am forever grateful to the county health department for this group—they gave me a chance to see that life was still possible for me. Life wasn't over—it was just beginning.

I've marched in a few pride parades and been to a couple "Gay Days" at the area amusement park. We are such a strong, beautiful, talented, creative people!!! Most of my connections now are through my work for youth advocacy and the occasional writing for lesbian news and literary magazines, but when pride month rolls around, I'm out there with the rest of the "family"!

Lisa Campbell

Right now I'm involved in a gay softball league. My fiancée has joined that league too. She'd come to a couple of games, and she sat in the dugout a few times. And she finally decided to join. I haven't really had much time to do any other projects, but I'm probably gonna get back into doing that. I'm moving to Vacaville, California. There's one gay bookstore. That's closing soon. I haven't really seen too much there. I'm gonna look for some more resources, though, and try to figure out ways to work with youth out there; it's so needed.

The first time I went to a youth group, I got there late 'cause I got kinda lost. I had an inadequate map. I had a friend give me a map, and it had a big section missing. I didn't have any clue how to find Telegraph Avenue. I hadn't been to Berkeley very much. The first time I walked in I was like, "Okay." Then somebody else came in after me, so I felt a little bit better. We both had to do introductions, and it was her first time at any youth group as well. So it was, "Okay, this is okay. I am not the only one who's new to this." There were probably about ten to fifteen people, somewhere in there.

After I'd left, I just felt like a huge weight had been lifted off me. I felt really good. I was feeling really good that day. And I remember, I went home, and two days later, a head gasket on my car blew. So my car was in the shop for two weeks. I couldn't get to therapy, and I couldn't get to this group. I called the therapist on the phone a couple of times, 'cause she said to just check in with her while I couldn't go. So that was cool.

I found out about this group, the Pacific Center, from my friend Evan; it was also spread around by word of mouth that this group was out there, so I just showed up. They talked about all these presentations and stuff that they wanted to do. And I asked a teacher at my school working with the Pacific Center, "Are you gonna have a student involved in doing some of the speaking too, because it makes a bigger impact if you have someone who's their own age, or close to that age." He hadn't really thought about that, and since no one else was really brave enough to do it, I did it. Nobody else wanted to do it, but I didn't mind. It was something I was willing to do.

I didn't want to come into the youth group and just take over. There were as many as eight people who would show up. It's just a thing where it wasn't really advertised too much. More might have shown up if it had been advertised. But then you might have gotten a few gay bashers outside too.

I went for over a year, pretty much. And after I started dating, I got away from it a little while, and then I'd go on occasion. And right now, I'm living over in Vacaville, so it's quite a drive. So I haven't gone in a while. But a lot of the people have changed, the facilitator's changed, and it's just a different atmosphere now. To some extent it's better because it's attracting more people, but I'm kinda used to the other way.

I feel a different connection with queer youth than I do with other kids or adults. Like a family connection. With the youth, we know what one another has gone through. We understand it. Straight youth . . . they can sympathize, but they don't all the way understand what it's like to be called "queer" and all these names in derogatory ways. They just don't understand. But with my queer friends, we really understand one another like that. We try and help one another out solving problems and stuff.

Mathis

When I was little, I had a lot of black friends. Sometimes that connection depends on where you're from, but, if you're in the middle of America, in Oklahoma, whenever black people see other black people, sometimes they just walk up to them, don't even know who they are. Sometimes you can't tell, sometimes you can, with gay people. And if you can, I always end up going up and talking to somebody. Like last night on the bus on the way home. I was on a city bus, and the bus driver was being mean to this girl and another girl who was with her. I assume it was her girlfriend. He was harassing her, and I identified with her, so I started talking to her, and I found out she was a lesbian.

I feel a different connection with queer youth than with other kids or even adults. It's like they're family. Some people have a lot of friends; some of them are straight, some of them are gay, some of them are bi, and some of them are nothing. But I really feel closer to the gay ones. There's just so much in common that you can't ignore that you have a connection. I think it's because we share the same experiences. It's almost like we have a connection through all of this, a very unique connection.

I'm a member of a youth group, Positive Images, which is a lot of fun. I've met a lot of people. At first, it was really hard there because I fell in love with this guy, but it was just a very sour situation. Another guy is in love with him, and now I'm falling in love with the guy who is actually in love with him. Well anyway,

I'm the secretary of the youth group. I have done a lot with that group, just supporting other people's decisions, doing some of the footwork for them. I also publish in our group magazine, *Images.* The first pieces were exclusively mine. After it started circulating, people totally raved about it. Straight people were totally thinking it was great and everything, but I let my cousin who lives with me read it. She told me she thought it was gay pornography. That hurt so much. She just could not relate to it.

Michael Talis

Besides the gay/straight group at my school, Rainbow Alliance, I know of no other types of support groups. I'm not even a member of the Rainbow Alliance because I'm fearful of my friends' reactions.

This is why I was struggling with this issue for so long: I had no one with whom I could talk about it. I found the soc.support.youth.gay-lesbian-bi newsgroup on-line and it made a world of difference. I owe my recent enlightenments and other stuff to the members of the newsgroup.

I would like to get involved with many homosexual-type groups, but I'm still very worried about tipping off my parents/friends/family to my homosexuality. So I still try to lay low.

Mary Toth

Before I found a gay youth support group, my main outlet was mailing off to bookstores, lesbian publishers and things like that, and getting catalogs and ordering books. Books were how I survived. I fed on books. That entire summer I was coming out, I swear I read 200 books on being lesbian. I was just all, "Munch!"

Then I started regularly going to a support group. That was kind of weird because my parents were driving me down there, and it was the time when I had my learner's permit but I didn't have my driver's license yet. My mom kept bugging me about having my driver's license. And she'd say, "I'm not gonna take you to group until you get your driver's license." I freaked out. And it was only group that they wouldn't take me to. Fuck, this is my only method of support.

I finally got my driver's license, and I was just never home. I would stay out at Aroma's, the Santa Rosa coffeehouse where most of the dykes hung out; I'd stay there forever trying to find a girlfriend. I was just on a search.

Folks at the support group would go and talk to particular groups of people. We did a panel for a human sexuality class at Sonoma State University. We also did a panel for a bunch of teachers—I don't remember what particularly—and other high schools, colleges, counselors, support service people, things like that. And then I also did a panel at my own high school, which was kinda hard.

Things at home were really stressful, being in school, pressure from my parents. Having the support group was weird because, being the only child and being the social outcast that I was, I didn't feel like I had anybody. Having a network of people with whom I could talk about my problems and things like that was so new for me. Before, I'd been sent to school counselors as the problem child, but I would sit there and be silent and morose the entire time. The counselors generally talked to my parents about the fact that I was going on about how much they fought, or they'd send me back to class thinking it was a waste of my time.

Now I had this support group, which was just an amazing eye-opener for me; I wanted to get into therapy and stuff like that. My parents, however, were always sort of antitherapy. So that support group made a big difference in my life.

Paige

I'm involved with the Billie deFrank Center. I went to Billie deFrank, and it was the first support group for queer youth I went to. They have a youth group for ages fourteen through seventeen. Well actually before that, I got a friend to go to the Billie deFrank Bingo with me on a Wednesday night. But then after that, I went to a youth support group—I think they called it a youth rap or something—I thought it was really lame.

I think I was beyond that. I felt I was definitely more mature. So I talked to the woman who ran it afterward, and I'm like, "I'd really like to participate in something like this because it would give me kind of an outlet, but I just feel like I'm really not for this group." I think it might have actually been the right level of maturity for the people there. I just felt I was beyond that. I think it shouldn't be so much based on age but just kind of getting people together, have one big group and then see who splits off. Whoever feels most comfortable. I was talking to other sixteen-year-olds, and I'm like, "This is not what I need." I think it should be based on your level of maturity more so than your age. But I can't imagine ever being out at twelve.

I went after that to an eighteen-to-twenty-three group, and I felt a lot more in place just 'cause of my maturity level, I think. Through that, I got to talk about stuff that was going on in my life, stuff that was going on with my parents. It gave me an outlet for my anger and my frustration.

Then there's the place in Santa Cruz. I don't know what the exact name of it is, but it's right behind Main Street in Santa Cruz. They run a youth support group. I also work with Aris Project in San Jose, but it's not exactly gay/lesbian youth. It goes out into homes for AIDS-related things. We cook meals; we give support, things like that.

In Massachusetts, I'm vice president of the Bi, Gay, and Lesbian Association on my campus. I think I got into it because I was interested in meeting some of the gay youth on campus. I don't know; I wasn't going into it as an activist or for support, just purely to meet people, and I met some really great people in it. Hopefully, next semester, being vice president, I'll be able to get a lot more done. I'd like to see a lot more done. I'd like to see some type of pride month. It doesn't have to coincide with anything else. Just a couple of activities that would definitely get us out there. We did a few things last year: we did a safe-sex dance and then an S&M lecture, and we celebrated National Coming-Out Day. Those things went off very well. I did the youth parade in Boston just recently. That was really neat. I marched in that with a couple of friends from school. But I'd like to be taken a little bit more seriously. I'd like to go after a little more serious type of event.

Todd Fay-Long

I marched in the Sonoma County parade, and that was really cool. And then I went to the San Francisco parade and marched in that. I was just really active; it was June; it was Gay Pride Month and all this fun stuff. And I was in this cool youth group. I led this brainstorming committee in our youth group. And then I ended up becoming copresident of my youth group. And so I did that.

With queer kids I meet outside of the youth group, it's the only thing we have in common is that we're gay and we're young. They just go to clubs and get fucked up and have sex all the time. They go down to the Castro and pick up guys. And I know it's their internalized homophobia and that kind of stuff, and they're dealing with that. But at the same time, they don't do anything with their lives, and I just can't relate.

I marched in my town in the Veteran's Day Parade with the Sonoma County Gay and Lesbian Pride Organization because I'm on the board of directors. That was really a trip because we got booed by some people, and some people were like, "Yeah, right on!" It was so cool being in my hometown, in this dinky little parade, and I could totally yell back when we got heckled. That was a trip.

In September, the youth in Positive Images put on this dance called the Homecoming Out. It was a gay youth dance, the first gay youth dance in Sonoma County. Right around then, I just decided that I wasn't going to stay with my dad anymore, he wasn't supportive of me, and I couldn't live in his environment. I didn't have my own room; I shared a room with his office, 'cause he worked at home, so I couldn't have any gay things out, or anything like that. He was very judgmental of my friends; he just really stereotyped my friends in certain groups. So I packed up and moved in with my mom.

I was going to Santa Rosa Junior College. I was just really busy. I was taking eighteen units, which is a lot. I was working, I was teaching art at the school that I graduated from, and I was working for this event coordinator, serving at weddings and parties and stuff like that. The event coordinator I worked for was really cool. I got that job through my youth group, 'cause he called and said they were looking for people to work. Everyone I worked with was gay, and he's gay, and it's really fun, and I still work there sometimes. I was just really busy, I was doing stuff with my youth group and being in their leadership and that kinda stuff. I felt really alive.

Jim

I haven't really heard of any youth organization support groups for gay kids. I haven't really looked into it.

Chapter 10

Is This Your First Time? First Kisses, Relationships, and Other Such Things

REMEMBER YOUR FIRST KISS?

Who can forget one's first kiss, the rush of puppy love, the tribulations of tending a broken heart? These are memorialized and celebrated moments in the United States. Whether one actually goes through these experiences or bears witness to them, one assumption is pervasive and unchallenged: the actors playing out these moments are unquestionably heterosexual.

In the United States, the passage from childhood to adolescence is often marked by the onset of puberty. Cultural space is made to accommodate this growth, although it is almost without exception heterosexist. Schools hold dances, awkwardly attended by preteenage boys and girls. They are encouraged to seek out a "nice boy" or a "nice girl" by their parents, teachers, and each other. A tremendous amount of social pressure sends conflicting messages, expecting chaste, modest behavior and sexual exploration at the same time.

But the development of sexuality has never socially condoned the questioning of one's sexual identity. Young men and young women uninterested in members of the opposite sex were considered late bloomers, shy. If the lack of interest continued, a questioning of the young person's sexuality was almost certain to follow.

It seems ironic that the process of exploring sexuality has become so taboo. It is so common for young men, whether straight or gay, to experience sexual feelings while playing with other boys. Boys talk (at the very least) about their sexual fantasies and arousal.

Young women are no less likely to participate in this kind of group exploration, "practicing" kissing and cuddling with their female friends. It only becomes an issue when young people stop playing and seriously turn their attentions to someone of the same gender as themselves.

For older queers, this meant that many of their first sexual experiences were efforts to make themselves straight or that they denied themselves any sexual pleasure for fear their queer desires would be exposed. For young men, opportunities to explore queer sexuality led them to public parks, rest rooms, or other places where they had heard men met to have sex with one another. No doubt, this informal network existed to some extent for queer women as well, but it has received far less notoriety.

The weight attached to such anonymous sexual encounters is difficult to assess. For many, such opportunities were probably the few moments of sexual fulfillment they were able to find. For others, it may have had a negative impact on their perception of intimacy as something to be experienced in sexual exploration with a trusted partner.

With the burst of queer visibility, particularly among queer young people over the last decade, youth are now, more than ever before, finding one another at early ages, perhaps at the time in their lives when they are first recognizing their queer sexual desires.

It is still the norm, however, for queer youth to have to hide the rush of their first kiss or heavy crush from their peers and families. They are expected to be ashamed of their sexuality and certainly not expected to "flaunt" it by carrying on a relationship in public.

School dances such as the senior prom epitomize the pressures placed upon young people to find romance and present that relationship to their peers and families. There are some great stories from the young people here describing their prom experiences and the rush of queering that cultural celebration of heterosexuality.

Whether one can look back fondly on memories of young love, or whether it is something that never seemed to come around, it is revitalizing to experience the passions of young queer love through the voices of the young people here. They remind us all that much of what we struggle for in our efforts toward queer liberation is in the name of love.

* * *

Adam Hardy

Pat had been subtly coming on to me for some time, and he quit entirely when he found out I was gay. My first few tentative sexual experiences were with Pat, and both were horrendously bad and thankfully short and interrupted. Several of my friends describe the things Pat did to me at the time as serious mental (if not sexual) abuse, so I'll leave you with their impression. I, for my part, have had friends who were abused in a much worse manner than I was, and the effects of the things Pat did to me, while unhealthy, don't haunt me like many of my friends are haunted.

I believed I was in love with Pat for a long time before I realized that I didn't love him, I didn't like him, and I actually sort of hated him. I think I believed I loved him because he didn't immediately reject me when I came out to him. Pat also fooled around with my best friend, Lewis, which pretty much mangled my emotions. Shortly after Pat tried to seduce one of my straight friends, I told him, quite politely, to get the hell out of my life and not come back.

When I stood up to Pat, I think it gave me a better grasp on myself and I achieved another level of self-confidence. Despite (or perhaps because of) the hell that Pat put me through, I had grown stronger.

Lewis and I fooled around sometime over that summer. The word "bisexual" came up afterward. A few weeks later, I came out to him as gay, which was rather difficult. The funny thing was, Lewis was surprised and disconcerted when I told him. This became increasingly stranger when we ended up in bed together ten minutes after I told him.

After every time we fooled around, he'd sort of punish himself (or me) by not speaking to me for a week or so afterward. Inevitably we'd end up in bed together. The situation was complicated when I told him I was in love with him. For some time, Lewis remained the only friend I had who knew about me, and we had something of a psychotic relationship, with me being the "other man" he cheated with on all his girlfriends. It was actually a pretty bad thing, but at least I was out to someone. Our sexual encounters were always one-sided and always brief. Strangely, I think they were killing me as much as saving me.

I guess a lot of gay teenagers must miraculously find one another, but I never really did. Lewis and I never went anywhere. Our sexual relationship, such as it was, ended, and has only resurfaced on occasion. We're still close friends, but we've developed a unique, intense love for each other that encompasses a lot of things, but not really romance. Other than him and a bisexual friend named Ted, I didn't know any available guys, and the emotional (not to mention sexual) need for another guy was driving me into fits of depression. When you're a gay teenager, you don't get to date like straight kids, and while the rest of my being was growing rapidly, my development as a sexual/romantic being was stunted.

Much to my chagrin, there were only three noncloseted gay men on my school's campus at the time I arrived here—myself and San and Nick, the couple. I went through a phase when I got here of utter elation over being out of the closet, where I'd talk about being gay endlessly, and I think I annoyed more than a few people with my single-mindedness.

Interestingly, things finally began happening for me romantically that semester when I got back home for my breaks. I went on my first date with a guy named Steve whom I'd met through one of my college friends. It wasn't particularly happy—Steve only wanted me physically—and it didn't make me feel any more closely connected with the "gay community," whatever that was. Steve was only interested in the sexual side of being gay—he promised to teach me "cruising spots," something I never took him up on. Steve didn't really want much to do with me after that date. I went out with a sweet guy from Tennessee after that, who was quite chivalrous and didn't push any sexual envelopes.

I've yet to be in a relationship, though I'd very much like one. It's *still* a problem for me to meet other gay and bisexual guys my age. I've met a guy at home via an on-line newsgroup I'm on who wants to put together a gay youth group in my hometown, and I intend to help him do so.

I've developed an aversion to bars, from what I've heard about the sexualization of gay culture there. The weird thing is that when you finally get some self-esteem about being gay, you have to unlearn all these things about gay men that you've been taught. However, you end up growing older and learning that lot of it was *true!* A lot of gay men out there just want sex, and that's not easy for a young hopeless romantic to deal with.

Alan Wiley

My first crush was probably when I was in elementary school. I used to have little crushes on girls 'cause I thought I was supposed to. I remember thinking, "I'm gonna marry so-and-so," or whatever. But at the same time, I'd go out and kiss my best friend—who was a boy—on the mouth in the middle of the playground. In elementary school, first grade through third grade, I would totally kiss my best friend on the mouth, in front of everyone, in front of my parents, teachers, all the other kids.

I had one relationship with a girl in junior high that lasted for three years, and the most I ever did with her was kiss her on the cheek. I could not stand her; I hated her. I just felt like that's what I was supposed to be doing. When I was a sophomore in high school, I went out with a senior, and she was really, really pretty, and she was very nice, and all the boys wanted her. And I just thought that I probably should too. She was a cool person, and I just wanted to be friends with her. So I went out with her for about a month, and that didn't go anywhere either. She knows I'm gay now. But I never had that much interest in having a relationship with women as far as a girlfriend kind of relationship goes.

I've had next to no sexual experience. My earliest sexual experience was probably sometime in junior high, maybe. I've never had sex, still to this day, just for my own personal reasons. Not necessarily religious or moral or ethical. It's just not what I want to do right now.

I've had three boyfriends in my life. One of them was in high school, and he was fifteen, and we would kiss and stuff. And then I had one in college when I first got to college, and that just totally didn't work out. And I've got one now, and we just hang out. I don't know, being gay isn't about sex for me. Being gay is about falling in love. And, yes, there's definitely the physical thing going on there, with the attraction. But it's so much more a mental thing for me. Like the way straight people could not fall in love with a person of the same sex necessarily, I just don't feel like I could fall in love with a woman.

At the same time, I have close emotional bonds with women. My best friend is a girl, and I plan on having children with her some day, just 'cause we're so much on the same level. She's very open-minded, and we love each other in the sense that we're best friends and we're very compatible. But I could never fall in love with her, and there's just not any physical thing going on there. I would never have sex with her or anything. It's about falling in love with people, and I just happen to fall in love with guys. I always have.

I was always falling for straight guys in school. It was so hard. I would become such close friends with someone and love them in the sense of being a friend. And then something would happen, and I would start to fall in love with them; I had to seriously stop myself from doing that. It was work. And I would just have to tell myself, "Look, he's straight; don't even think about it." But that's hard sometimes. Especially with my friend Matt who lived with me. He was living with me and my family, and he'd known that I was gay for about a year and a half before he lived with me. He was my best friend. He needed a place to live, so he lived at my house. He's straight, but I had fallen in love with him years earlier, and I just wanted to be close to him. I don't know, it never really played into our relationship that much, because he was not gay. So I would keep trying to convince myself that he was gay, and it just didn't work out.

The first reason I even talked to him was because he had few friends and I thought he was cute, and I told myself, "I'm gonna be best friends with this guy within a month." And I was. We would hang out all the time; I showered him with attention, and no one had ever done that for him before. I felt kinda bad because I went into that relationship thinking, "I want this guy; he's really hot." After a couple weeks, after we started to get to know each other, I dropped that attitude, and we became great friends. But it was hard. I struggled for about three years with the fact that he wasn't gay. I did not want to deal with that. I wanted to believe he was gay.

Eileene Coscolluela

Well, here at the university, I live in a dorm. During the weekends at school, I live with my boyfriend in his apartment. I've been dating him since I've been here at the university (a year and a half), and it looks like we'll be dating for a *very* long time. I cannot deny that I have feelings for women, but I don't think I'll ever have a relationship with a woman. I'm very monogamous and don't have any desire to be with a woman sexually right now and think I'll be with my boyfriend for a long time.

Dawn McCausland

So here I am, gung ho; I'm coming out. I met this girl who was a friend of a friend of mine, and we started hanging out. I started to get a crush on her, and she and I began hanging out alone; it was getting close to Valentine's Day. She wasn't making a move, and I was getting anxious because I tend to be very ambitious. So I decided that I would ask her out for Valentine's Day, even though I'd never done anything with a woman in my life, including kiss one, in a girlfriend manner.

I painted this little picture, and I did this nice calligraphy stuff. I gave her a daisy and this chocolate bar. I remember I was so damn nervous, and she almost didn't show up to meet me in between classes. I was so freaked out. I thought, "What if she rejects me and she doesn't like me?" So I gave it to her, and I just remember sitting on the second story of the building watching her down below, watching her unpack the entire thing and read it and just kinda sit there and ponder it. I was sitting there wondering, "What's she thinking, what's her expression? Oh, I wish I could see her; what's going on, what's going on?!"

The next twenty-four hours were so stressful waiting for her to reply. Finally she said, "Yeah, sure." It was totally casual for her. I was like, "I got my first girl date!" I was running around the house, and getting all these congratulations from my family members. Oh, I was baby dyke from hell. She was only, I guess, two years older than me. She was eighteen at the time; I was sixteen. So then the night before we're supposed to go out for Valentine's Day, we and a couple of other friends go out to the beach, this whole thing under the stars, and we cuddle up next to the fire and we kiss. Nothing else happened, but it was just so romantically cute, like the perfect little first date and first kiss. I just remember the feeling: she kissed me and then I pulled back and I kind of got in this little ball. "I just want to sit here and savor this. I don't want her to kiss me again. I've gotta process this. I have to hang on to this, this is so precious."

I don't know, it was just so amazing. It was so genuine, it was so tender, it was so—I don't know. It was incredible. My journal entries from that night are just hilarious: "It was so amazing, and then she touched my hand, and then she touched my hair, and then I laid in her lap in the car on the way home." There was all this lovey-dovey, I don't want to say overreacting, but everything was just like ten times more dynamic than it would usually be.

So then the next day, we went on our first little date, and that was the first time I ever messed around with a girl. I called my mother, and I said, "Can I stay another hour?" I came home at 4:00 in the morning on a school night. I had such a divine crush on this girl, and I just wanted this girlfriend so bad. A lot of it had to do with her, because she's an incredible person. But a lot of it just had to do with the experience of a girl.

But things didn't last with us because she was in another relationship, and it was obvious, especially since she was my first girlfriend, I was not gonna be able to handle an open relationship. I was too possessive, and I just wanted her all to myself. I even remember driving home after our first actual date, saying to myself, "Don't jump to conclusions now; it's just your first girlfriend."

I was trying to stay in the box that I had defined for myself previous to that. And then I started to inch away from that, and I started to realize that I didn't really like guys. I hadn't dated guys in a long time. My last relationship with a guy was pretty dysfunctional. Not in a bad sense, not like he raped me or it was horribly passive-aggressive or anything. But I wasn't fully there. My feeling wasn't in it. So I seemed to realize that there was a total disparity in my feelings for both boys and girls.

I got into a total psychoanalysis of whether or not I was gay. Those were probably the most humorous of my journal writings. I have an entire journal devoted to lists and comparative things and explanations of this and that. I still hang on to the fact that I had so many boyfriends that were so far away. I started to add it up, and it kind of looked unequal, you could say. Then I just said, "Well, fuck it, I'm not gonna analyze this anymore." I had a few more girlfriends, and just totally realized that that's what I identified with and I really didn't like guys as more than friends. I just liked cuddling, and I was very affectionate, and I liked hanging out with guys, and that was okay. I didn't have to hate men to be a lesbian.

As far as how my girlfriend Mary and I met, well, we had mutual friends, and we had seen each other around a lot. Anyway, I was going through a pretty hard time, and so I really wasn't looking for a girlfriend and sort of put her on the side. I had just moved into town, right next to our school—we go to school together at the junior college.

The beginning of the semester, I had decided to go over and pay for my first semester classes—this is about two months ago, I guess. And I got into line and happened to stumble behind an ex-boyfriend of mine in the accounting line, one that I was not especially fond of. I didn't want to sit for about twenty minutes in the line behind him. I decided to leave, and I came back about five minutes later, and Mary was the last one in line, and so I said to myself, "Okay, good, lesbian, I can deal with that." Well, she's got her school backpack on, and it's got a black triangle on the back of it. I joke with people at my work that our little gay buttons have some pretty practical purposes too. If we're gonna be in line together and she's cute, I might as well try to say something. So I came up with some dumb line: "Where did you get your button? I've been looking for one." Like I couldn't find one anywhere, of course. That's how it all began.

Eriq Chang

I've had girlfriends and boyfriends, but I'm not a player. The longest relationship I've had was actually five or six months with my boyfriend Mark. He's nineteen. I usually like people who are around my age or a little bit older. We met at the mall. I approached him in a weird manner, because at the time I was working on the printing of a book of pictures, and I was looking for models. So I approached him, and I said, "Would you like to help me with my book?" I'm totally a stranger, I know, but this is the best way for me to get to know someone. He agreed, and we basically got to know each other. We went out, and we started getting into deep talk, as though we sort of knew each other well. I still love him. He's a great guy. He's cool and I related to him really well. I still do, but we had our differences.

The girls I have gone out with have been high school age or a little bit older. I went out with this girl Jennay, and with her, it was just total attractiveness. I got to know her on a different level, and we became lovers. It's funny to say it, but we didn't really relate emotionally. So we sort of became fuck buddies. This was actually going on at the same time I was going out with Mark, so it was kinda bad.

I think I'm attracted to strong women. I think I like men for different things. In men, I look for personality, looks, and stuff. For women, it's not even attractiveness; it's almost a power. I think women are like animals, they're powerful. They are the huntress, the seductress, but they can also be totally smart. They're a whole package. That's stereotyping men too. It's weird. It's hard for me to explain. I picture both as equal, but then each sex has its own characteristics individual to it. I don't know. I guess I have a checklist of what I'm looking for.

Last night, I went out with someone I was very interested in. His name is Matt. He goes to this school right here across the town. He's eighteen. We were just kinda hanging out 'cause he thinks we're just friends, but I really want to get to know him better. I know he's either gay or bisexual; I know he likes women, but no straight guy's gonna talk about men like he does. I'm interested, but the thing about him is he acts stupid even though he's really smart, and I don't like that.

Kyallee Santanders

It was at my first youth group meeting, May 12, 1993, when I met Shay. I told her about what was going on in my life, and she just listened. She said she understood what the razor marks on my arms meant and the fight behind coming out. Over the next few weeks, we chatted over the phone and got to know each other. In a rare moment of bravery, I asked her out on a date.

The date was an awkward thing for me, but it allowed us to talk and to just be together. I brought her home, and just when I thought she was going to open the car door and get out, she leaned over and kissed me. I closed my eyes and tried to make sense of it. She asked if I was okay, and I said that I was, I'd just never been kissed by a woman before. She laughed and kissed me again—really kissed me—and my body woke up. All of a sudden, I felt very hot and very . . . alive. I didn't know what was happening, but I knew that I didn't want it to stop.

Shay and I dated for a month before her fear of hurting me overshadowed our relationship. I left reluctantly, happy to remain friends and thankful for the chance to learn about myself and discover that I truly did have a sexual side.

I turned my thoughts to Boulder, where I would be going to college. I graduated top of my class and was awarded enough scholarship money from various organizations (including the Teacher's Group, a group of gay and lesbian educators) so that, on August 18, 1993, I could leave my parents' house, determined never to come back.

Lisa Campbell

I thought I'd get married, some day, far, far away in a different galaxy. I never pictured myself marrying a man. I couldn't picture it. I didn't see anything I was interested in. After I came out, I wanted to get married and have kids and that sorta thing. My ex-girlfriend wasn't into that. She was the type of person who didn't believe in marriage. All the people she knows who are married are unhappy. But I know some people that she knows who are happy. She just doesn't look at it that way.

My ex was playing darts by the entrance of this bar we went to; I saw her, but I didn't really. I didn't think too much of it at the time at all. It was the blonde that she and some friends were playing darts with who caught my eye.

Well, my ex and I both ended up hitting on the same straight girl. My ex danced with her, and the floor started to get crowded so she moved in a little closer, and the blonde girl said something, and my ex said, "Fuck you!" and walked off the floor. Later on, I could swear the blonde girl kept looking in my direction, so I thought, "Okay, I'm gonna go ask her to dance." So I went over and asked her to dance. She said, "No." I'm like, "Okay." I was sitting down talking to a friend, "What the hell, is she straight or something?"

Then this other girl comes walkin' by. She looked my way. I was looking, and she kinda turns around after she's passed me, just wanting to see if I'm looking. She caught me . . . the first person who ever caught me looking. She asked me to dance, and we ended up kissing before we even knew each other's name. I found out later that her name was Debbie. We got off the dance floor and talked for a while. We really hit it off. We set up a date for the next day. We were gonna meet in the city and go hang out in Castro. She was a little bit embarrassed about meeting me the day after. She'd had a couple of shots of Jagermeister and knew she'd done some things the night before she probably otherwise wouldn't have. I was looking to play around for a little while when I met my second girlfriend.

My father knows I'm gay and after me and my current girlfriend got engaged, I said, "You gotta meet him—if he finds out I'm married and I didn't tell him, he's gonna flip!" I called his house, I set up a dinner with him, and we went out to dinner after I got off work. My fiancée was nervous as hell, because she just figured they're gonna think this old woman [she's in her early thirties] is preying on their daughter or something. But my folks and she kinda hit it off. They get along fine. The only thing now to do is tell them that we're engaged.

My stepmom's parents know that I'm living with my girlfriend. They don't know that I'm engaged. My dad doesn't know that I'm engaged either yet. None of my family know. My girlfriend and I have only been dating a couple of months, and so they might think that's quite an irresponsible decision of me. Debbie, my fiancée, is thirty-one and I'm eighteen.

If the two people involved really care about each other, and it's a quality relationship, and it's not one person taking advantage of the other person, then it's okay. I've noticed in the queer community that there are a lot of couples with age differences, a lot of big age gaps.

If there's more for youth to do together, they don't have to always go out with older people. It may lessen the age difference in the community. The person that's right for them may still be that older person, but then at least they get some dating experience with someone younger—their own age or mental level.

Mathis

In *Steel Magnolias,* I know it's corny, but there was this one line that stuck out to me. Olympia Dukakis said, "That which does not kill us only makes us stronger." And for me, that was just so true. Because now I feel that I have such mental strength. Going through what I did with my stepfather molesting me while I was growing up just taught me that my physical body can withstand anything.

I just wish that I could have lost my virginity the way I wanted to. You can't ignore what's actually happened, but I think I would have lost my virginity probably around fourteen or fifteen if I had the choice. But I would do it with someone I wanted to lose my virginity with. I don't feel ashamed talking about the fact that I've been molested or raped because I know that it's not my fault. I've always known that it's not my fault. Well, not always, sometimes I did blame myself. But I would really like to have an experience that I could actually tell people and be very, very proud of.

And now I'm learning that my heart can withstand a lot. Actually, my heart can withstand being hurt a lot easier than it can feeling joy and emotion. To me, life was just sex. Sex is fine, actually quite good, but that's not what it's all about. We have to have some substance to our relationships. You have to have somebody who cares about you.

Loving somebody you actually want to love is the most important thing to me. You have to love your mother because she's your mother. But you don't have to love other people. And the best part of being gay is being able to love somebody you want to love.

A girl and I who met at a friend's slept together. We didn't have sex, but we slept together. She was very affectionate. She was hurt at the time; and she needed somebody to be close to. I was just kind of watching myself and looking at my feelings while things were happening and stuff, for changes in my feelings. I really didn't expect anything to happen, and it didn't. I was kind of wondering. But I know I'm gay.

Mary Toth

I decided to join a support group. That happened over a Christmas break, oh, two years ago or so; I can't remember. I was about fifteen, I think. I was young. I was really jazzed about going to this queer support group. I got the number from a friend of mine who was in peer counseling, and I did the group's little intake meeting. The group's name is Positive Images. So now I had a new gay person in my life, the lesbian who had done my intake. We hung out a bit; we hung out at the beach, and that's where I had my first lesbian kiss; that kind of made an impression.

At the beach, under the full moon—it was very odd. I think I almost fell over. It was very funny! But I wasn't even particularly attracted to the person. Yet I was thinking, a woman kissing me now . . . Cream! Then we processed the kiss all the way back into town from Goat Rock Beach into Santa Rosa, back to the coffeehouse, asking ourselves, "What does this mean?" She then broke up with me at the coffeehouse that night. She said, "I'm seeing somebody else right now, and I'm not sure if we want to open our relationship." So that was my introduction to the wide world of lesbians.

I got my first girlfriend at Aroma's. Every girlfriend I've gotten, basically, I've got at Aroma's, the local coffeehouse/queer hangout. She was going to Sonoma State University. We went to the March on Washington together, with our support group. So my first girlfriend and I hung out a lot; she was older and she had run away from home from some pretty severe abuse stuff.

I'm with the raddest woman now. We met at the JC—I had just gotten out of bed, and this was my one thing for the day: I have to go pay my fees; I know they're late. So I stumble out of bed, I'm weary, I'm in my jammies, and I've just been slut girl of the century for the past six months. I am so hardened. I'm stumbling into this accounting line, totally oblivious. We started all scamming on each other; I'm all, "Oh, cute dyke!" But being the nerd that I am, I don't even know she's hitting on me. No, she's too cute. Of course, she wouldn't hit on me. I was just so oblivious.

Paige

Heidi's my girlfriend. She's incredibly supportive. I think that's what really attracted me to her. We met in Modesto, California. Don't be scared now; she's not from there. She's the friend of one of my close family friends. We met and we were just kind of chatting, and when she moved to San Jose she gave me a call and said, "Oh, will you show me around the Bay Area?" I showed her around, and she was talking to me about how she's a lesbian and how she was coming out, and just started talking. I went off to school, and we kept on talking. We just really, really get along.

In my hometown, I hear the whispers when we're out in public, and I think "It's your problem." My dad knows who she works for. He knows her and we go out to lunch. My dad's a lot more open about it.

I'm glad that he's cool with it. Heidi and I are a lot alike, and so it's really nice to have someone like that. And I think it was just that—snap!—you know what's going on and you know it's right.

Todd Fay-Long

I was dating this twenty-five-year-old guy. But then we broke up, because I was messing around with this other guy who was a friend of his, this twenty-seven-year-old, and I was only sixteen. It wasn't really a right thing, I don't think, because I knew they were only attracted to me because I was young, and it wasn't even like they were attracted to me because of my personality or anything like that. So I dated the twenty-seven-year-old for a little bit, and then we broke up, and I got back together with my old boyfriend, and then we broke up again.

When I was with my first boyfriend, we went to a rave; I felt like we could dance together and stuff, and we could kiss and it was cool. But I still felt kind of weird. I used him. And when I was with him, I was really out. I would hold hands everywhere, kiss in public. But it wasn't so much that I wanted to be kissing him as much as I wanted to be able to be that out; I wanted to get comfortable with it.

I met this one guy in the city, and he came up with us, back up to Petaluma, and we hung out that night. We just totally talked. He was this really cool person. We had sex, and it was really good—five hours of foreplay. That was rad, and I just felt like I could talk to him, like we could really relate. So he came back down to the city, and then I called him that night, or I called him the next day or something, and asked him to come up, and so he rode the bus up, stayed at my house that night, and we had sex again.

He was just rad; he had the body type that I like, a little pale and kind of scrawny—kinda skaterish, like a toned-all-over body. Anyway, so then he went back to the city, and I was supposed to come down to the city and stay at his house on Friday. I called his house and his roommate said, "Maddy doesn't live here anymore; he went back to Michigan." He never called me, and he's never called me or written me since then. It was really fucked. I even think that I am in love with him because I just think about him every day. I don't even know if I've ever been in love before this.

I've set an age limit of twenty for myself, and I'm gonna try not to date anyone over twenty, because I don't feel like anyone older can relate on that level. So right now I'm kinda dating somebody. He's in my youth group, and he just joined two weeks ago. He's twenty and he goes to Sonoma State University. He's Salvadoran and moved from El Salvador twelve years ago. His name's Hector, and he's really cool. But he's not out to anyone. He's not out to any of his friends. We were going dancing at this café in Cotati where I live. Well, he came and picked me up, and I said, "Let's go to this other café." And he goes, "I don't know, a lot of my friends go there." And I said, "Well, I'm not gonna out you, you know I just want to go dance." So he went and it was fun, and some of my friends were there and stuff. I don't know. It's like we're having sex, but he doesn't want to commit.

Jim

I've only gone out with one girl whom I totally fell in love with. Her name's Cathy. And at first, I was this immature little tenth grader, and I didn't know the first thing about love; she taught me what it was; girls have so many emotions. I think guys do too. But she was the only person I know who really understood me.

I've never been with a guy yet. I was tempted once. I was in this store—a clothes shop or something. Well, this guy was looking at me and my friend pointed it out. I was gonna go up and talk to the guy, but the guy was twenty-something. He was good-looking, too. This was like a year and a half ago or something. I was really screwed up—not sure how I felt. I didn't say anything. I remembered going home and wishing that I had said something.

Chapter 11

The Future: Where Are You Going?

LOOKING TOWARD THE FUTURE

The opportunities available to openly queer people in the United States continue to grow as acceptance of queer folks becomes more widespread. Although in most states, it is still legal to discriminate against us in housing, on the job, and often in the schools, the youth in this collection were amazingly optimistic about what was available to them in the future.

Few of the young people felt that being queer would hold them back from their career goals, and many certainly planned on finding someone special, falling in love, and having children. All were committed to making political change for the betterment of the queer community a part of their life's work. They are also undaunted by needing to fight for what they feel they deserve.

There are an increasing number of resources available for queer and questioning youth to support them in achieving their goals. Federal grants seeking to address the disproportionately high rates of suicide, substance abuse, and homelessness among queer youth, have made their way to agencies established solely to serve queer and questioning youth.

Sadly, youth are rarely part of the evaluation process of the services established to meet their needs. They are not asked what works or what doesn't and tend to become numbers rather than voices. This is not always the wish of the service provider, but the unfortunate by-product of working with limited resources and strict grant deadlines. Taking the time to really assess what youth want or feel they need (let alone create structures that empower the youth to lead themselves) becomes a luxury rather than a priority.

With few exceptions, youth are treated as clients of such agencies, presumably seeking shelter from the psychological fallout of living in a homophobic society. Their needs, and by extension the youth themselves, are immediately pathologized. They are rarely seen as activists and leaders within the community and more rarely provided with resources to proactively change their circumstances. They are not empowered to shape their own destinies. Although the modern queer movement has come to recognize youth as a part of the community, it is still a battle for young people to represent their needs or put forth their visions of change for the future without being told to stand to the side and wait until they are given their time to speak. The impact is particularly defeating, for without hearing from the young constituents in need of these support services, it is unlikely their needs will be met. If these needs are not met somewhere along the line, their opportunities to reach the futures they imagine rapidly move further from their grasp.

The final questions the young people asked one another in the interview sessions that produced these narratives were, "What do you see for your future?" and "What would you like to say to folks out there—young or old, straight and queer?" Aside from wanting to hear what these young people saw for themselves, what they saw as possible for their community, I wanted to create some way for them to pass on their insights to those who may be reading this book. They really are the experts in where queer youth services should go, what the next steps should be, and I thought getting answers to these questions might prove useful to other youth, adult allies, and service providers alike.

The responses certainly reflect the unique experience and needs of each speaker, but some notable commonalities exist. Sharp criticisms are made of the adult queer community for the neglect of queer youth. Educators and others in positions of authority receive strong calls to action to intercede and support queer and questioning youth in school environments.

Most poignant to me, however, is how many of the speakers call out to other youth similar to them. Several people implore other youth questioning their sexuality to just be proud and love themselves for who they are, wanting them to know they are not alone, that there are others out there just like them. Valuable lessons are present in these final chapters, representing a vast breadth and depth of experiences. Their messages speak to why they all hold such exciting visions for what is possible not only for themselves but for others like them.

* * *

Anthony Gomez

After high school, I want to go to UC Davis. Either that or become a singer, because I've won awards for having a good voice. So either one is a choice for me. And another thing I want to do is go out there and try to help as many people as I can about being gay; educate them and educate the community better so they don't have this ridiculing attitude toward us.

I feel the next step toward gay liberation is marriage. That's what I'm hoping for. I'm hoping that we can marry, 'cause straight people can marry all they want. We should fight for our rights; we should not be treated unfairly. We should be treated equally.

I wish to have kids, but right now I'm not looking that far. I've been abused. I've been sexually molested and raped four times. I think I need to be stable before I can have kids or a family.

Adam Hardy

I've known since I was eight years old that I want to write and possibly draw comics for a living. I want to end up with a long-term relationship. I want to get married to the man I fall in love with, live maybe in Boston somewhere. We'll discuss having kids and perhaps adopt, if we feel that it would be a good thing. I'd like to do something like what Ivan Velez Jr. and other comics writers are doing right now, which is integrating gay characters into comics. I know that I looked up to comic book heroes when I was a kid, and I think that gay youth could use role models too. Mostly, though, I'm just looking at being happy, creating, and trying to live as good a life as possible.

I'm seeing homophobia disappear in younger teens these days. Quite frankly, it's becoming uncool. I want to help start that support group in my hometown, though, because it's going to take time for our society to heal this thing, and I want to make sure that as few people as possible go through the hell that I went through as a kid.

I know that I'm now living what I once thought was impossible—a happy, peaceful, content life as an openly homosexual person. I now consider being gay a gift, because I think it's forced me to grow and become a stronger, more compassionate individual, and through adversity, I think it's given me parts of myself I wouldn't have had otherwise. It's an amazing example, I think, of how your life is only what you make of it, and what you make of it can be wonderful.

Alan Wiley

I have really strong morals and ethics. Growing up in a religious home, you get that drilled into you. That's just what makes me happy: having that belief system of treating other people with as much kindness as you can. And to me, the whole reason I'm on Earth is to love other people and to make other people happy. So I just go with that. If I'm doing something that makes other people happy, that makes me feel happy; then I don't feel like I'm doing anything wrong.

I'm really into music. I love music. I've played the tuba for seven years, and I've played the bass guitar for seven years also. I love to record, I love playing music and being a part of music, and I'd like to do something in the music field. I enjoy writing also. So, I don't know; I really have no definite plans. I know I'd like to get married someday, and I'd like to have children someday.

Whenever I feel ready, I plan on getting married. Definitely a few years down the line. I want the white picket fence—I want it all. And I'm not gonna let anything stand in my way. I want a kid eventually. It would be nice to have children. I think I could be a good dad. And my parents played such an important role in my life, I want to be able to play that role in someone else's life. My parents were really incredible parents, and I love 'em to death. My parents are two of the finest people I know.

I hope that I can be a role model to other gay kids. I want to be more involved with the gay community, as much as I find a lot of things in the gay community disagreeable to my set of morals. I just want to get more involved in supporting people, because what life is about for me is about supporting people and having a positive effect on people's lives. I think you can really affect people more than you even know by being a good example, because I've had people who were good examples to me without them necessarily even knowing it. They have affected my life in such a strong way that I can't even express it really.

Eileene Coscolluela

I hope to be a professor or a researcher in the botanical sciences. I want to have a husband or partner—but most likely it will be a husband—and have a nice house and a good job that I'm happy at, but I don't think I want children. If I do have children, I would probably just want one.

I hope to remain active in glbt issues when I'm older, especially glbt youth. That's very important to me.

Dawn McCausland

I have a future of activism. That's a simple way of saying it. I'm finishing my last semester at the junior college, and I'm hoping to transfer to Mills College. I've gotten my acceptance letter, but I need my financial aid. So I hope to be going there. My major is kind of under sociology, but I want to study systems of oppression, which is like women's studies, ethnic studies, and urban studies, so I can study sexism, racism, and classism. And I'm sure, without a doubt, that homophobia will be in there. So I'm gonna be doing that, and I don't know who's gonna pay me to do what I want to do or what medium I'll do it through. I really want to work in social change and activism and education, probably write some books.

I'm sure I'll also be doing some revolutionary activity. So I expect to be popular and hated at the same time, like a good activist. So I expect to probably be assassinated. Activism is my top priority. I don't want a family. I don't want kids. I don't really care for kids. They seem like so much work and so much energy, and I'd be afraid I wouldn't like them. I'd be afraid I'd put too many of my wishes and desires and problems onto them. I'm afraid that I'd fuck them up. Honestly, I'm afraid that I'd be a bad parent, and I don't want some kid coming to me in therapy when he or she is fourteen years old, like I did to my mother, listing all the things that I did wrong. I'm a perfectionist, so I can't be a parent.

Eriq Chang

I want to own a multimedia company like Disney. But before that, I want to direct movies; I would love to direct movies and act. So far, I've been able to do artwork for computer games, LucasArts in Marin County. But I'm really trying to get my foot into the entertainment field. That's really where I want to go. Theater—not theatre, but movie theaters. I think that's the most powerful medium that you can use because it's on all emotional levels.

I don't really want a family. I'd love to be in a relationship with someone who is interesting. I'm not picky, but I need someone who is there when I need them there, but gives me space to work. I think in the field that I'm going into, it's very difficult until you're actually established and famous. If you are famous and you're bisexual or gay, like Madonna, you can get away with it and people can look up to you. But you give a part of yourself away when you're famous. I don't know if I'd be able to have a family and settle down, because I love to be busy.

Well, if I'm bisexual, I can't live in Oklahoma! I think I want to have an apartment in New York, a studio flat, and I want to have it lavishly designed by a top decorator. I'd love to live in Miami and LA. Three houses by the beach, and a flat in the city.

I'm looking at several different places for college. I really want to go to Fulsale, which is in Miami; it's an art school for recording, theatrical, and dramatic arts. Geena Davis and Madonna went there. It's an expensive school, but it's nice. They have the high-tech equipment, and they have contacts with the entertainment industry; UCLA, but it's difficult to get into the theater program; Cal Arts, which is a beautiful school too, right next to LA. LA is the center, the central place for entertainment—the place. I've heard terrible things about getting into the entertainment industry, "Blah blah blah." But I think that if you have talent and you can put it out there, that you can do it.

I'm scared about graduating. I'm really scared because I'm leaving a lot of people who are my friends, not really personal, personal friends, but people who have been there for me. I think the scariest thing is actually moving on with my life, finding out what I am gonna do, finding colleges and stuff. And that's scary. I really want to do all these things, but it's hard for me to get the willpower to actually apply somewhere. I'm afraid I won't be accepted. But I think that comes along with the territory about fears of being accepted by people. I am excited about my future, but I'm scared to leave the past. That's normal, I think.

Ernie Hsiung

I want to find that "perfect guy" as much as the next gay guy. I guess growing up the way I have has made me want the idea of the traditional family, with a wife, three kids, a job, and a picket fence. Being gay, I wouldn't be able to have that, and that's my biggest fear, something I'll have to work out throughout my life.

I see myself in a monogamous relationship, with a good job, a decent house, maybe a kid, somehow. I just want to be able to live my life simply, with someone.

Kyallee Santanders

I'm an engi-nerd, and I want to build and fix computers. Other than that, I'm pretty boring—I want a wife and a few kids and a house and a dog and a cat—you get the idea. I'm still young enough to be naive and think that I can do whatever the hell I want—why should my sexuality be a barrier?

I don't understand homophobia; I don't understand the lies and the hatred and the violence. When will we learn to look beyond the differences and realize that we are all more alike one another than we are unlike one another? And who the hell has the right to tell me what I can and can't do simply because I choose to share my life with a womyn and not a man?!

Lisa Campbell

I want to definitely take some gay literature classes and stuff like that. I want to learn more about the history too. That's one thing the youth doesn't learn about, gay history. And it's very important to know your past so you can figure out where you're going. I don't know any gay person my grandparents' age. I don't think many queer people my age do. But it's a link that needs to be made.

I want to be able to get one of those big ranches. Maybe forty acres or whatever, and having horses and kinda isolated from a lot of other people. That's something I would like in a home. I don't want to have neighbors who are so close that they can just look through the window and say, "Ah, yes, they're out there on their patio . . . . What are they doing?"

If I were gonna start a youth group in Vacaville, where I'm moving, I'd have a few objectives. One, to just help people with coming out. Two, to have support there, just have places for them to go and meet people. There's not really many places for youth to meet one another. And that's a big issue. If youth can meet one another, they can help one another out. That'll help the suicide rate drop. That's a very important thing for me. I would like to help get that down. It's senseless for kids to kill themselves. I was one of them, so I understand.

A lot of youth think, "Well, I'm just weird; there's nobody like me." But if you meet other people like you, you're more accepting of yourself; it makes it easier for you to come out. And also, it's fun to be around people who are like you, people who understand where you're coming from. On the social end, it's easier to get a date if you know people who are like you.

Mathis

I have no earthly idea what I'm gonna be doing in the future. That's what I've been having to think about a lot, because my aunt and uncle are asking me for some answers, and I don't have them; I don't know what I want to do.

When I was younger, I knew what I wanted to do, and now I just have no idea. But I know in the immediate future I want a very healthy relationship, because I've never really had a healthy relationship. The closest I've had was with a guy that I met at the lake when we lived in Davenport. I just met him at the lake, and he already had a boyfriend and stuff. I just walked up to him and said, "Do you want to fuck?" and we did. For a week. And then I went home because I couldn't handle it anymore. The relationship I had with my cousin was very, very twisted, and I didn't like hiding it. I mean, he was my cousin, and so it feels rather disgusting. But I think that you're gonna fall in love with whomever you're gonna fall in love with. I just really want a healthy relationship, instead of having to hide and wondering if somebody's boyfriend is behind my back, waiting to kill me or something. I just want a very loving romantic relationship. That's what I want in the future. That's the only thing I have picked out. But I know as long as I want one, I'm never gonna get one.

I'm just slowly moving on with my life. My aunt and uncle think that I should be moving much, much more quickly than I am. Now I have primarily gay friends. I have some straight friends. I really don't get along with them the way I wish I could, but I don't get along with them at all hardly. I don't get along with very many straight people, period. I really feel that they just don't have compassion for me; they don't really care. It's kind of interesting to realize that my life has been so twisted in the past and everything, but I still have huge problems trying to deal with normal obstacles and stuff through friendships and everything.

I think that if I do something in my future, the queer community will definitely be part of that. I do a lot of artwork, and it's very influenced by my sexuality.

I'm getting my GED next month. I'm going to go to the junior college here. I don't know what the hell I'm doing yet; I'm just going to take general stuff. I've been poor all my life, so making money in the future isn't that big of a goal; I've learned that I can live without money and be happy. I've come a really long way since I moved here.

Michael Talis

I want to be a journalist, either print or television, or a lawyer. I'm very interested in current events, and I like debating. I stay out of the math/science areas and stick to history, English, and French because I enjoy those subjects more.

There's several main reasons why I was hesitant in coming out to myself and admitting that I'm gay. One of the reasons was the thought of my adult life with a gay lover, but not a "family" in the usual sense. Is it healthy for two men to raise a child? For that matter, do they allow two men to adopt a child? I have big families on both sides and I enjoy family stuff tremendously. I want my own family with my lover to be as happy as I am in my family now. Is that possible being gay? God, I hope so.

I know I will definitely live in the city because of reasons mentioned elsewhere. Plus, being gay in a city is *easier* than being gay in the suburbs. My job won't be affected by my homosexuality.

Mary Toth

I'm going to school at the junior college. I plan on transferring somewhere, either Mills if I can or to a University of California campus. If I got to a school where I could, I would explore my more activist sides. That would be rad. But I'm a practical girl, and I realize that what I'm gonna do to be paying the rent for the rest of my life is probably not what I'm going to be doing as what I'd like my impact on the world to be.

I'm happy right now because I'm going to school and I'm working. I have the rad classes: Women and Social Change, African-American Literature. I'm really autonomous; I get to determine everything. So it just seems like this path that I finally get to start forging for myself; that's something that I've never had. I've always been told what to do. And so now, this is the first year where I get to decide whether or not I want to eat breakfast this morning. So everything's really new to me. I never really knew what I wanted before because nobody bothered to ask, but now I don't know what to do because I want to figure it out as I go along. I tend to be kind of spontaneous that way. I'm also spiffed out because I have a rad girlfriend right now, and she's real cute. She's helped me to realize that I want to do activism. She's like, "Oh, hi! You don't want to be a computer science major!" And I'm all, "Oh, thank you!" I've been waiting for someone to tell me that. So she's had a massive impact on my life already.

As far as what I want to be when I'm older? Hmm, that's a funny question. Well, as my day job, I do desktop publishing and graphic design. I've written some stuff. I have done writing for Macintosh-based computer magazines. I'm a Mac nerd, basically, by trade. So my day job is pretty much gonna be doing something like that. But really, what I want to do is see if I can get more into political activism and work toward that for the rest of my life. I want to either do that from the standpoint of direct action, like joining Queer Nation or Riot Grrls or chaining myself to something or marching all over the place.

Oh! I know: I want to be a Lesbian Avenger. That's what I want to be when I'm older. That's my aspiration, goddamnit. Either that or writing, because I've always felt a strong tie to writing.

A part of me really wants to have a family. I'm very maternal, which is kind of odd. Y'all should see a picture of me sometime. But I always wanted to have a kid. And now I'm not so sure. I always sort of had this ideal vision of having my primary partner—but we don't really live together; we just sort of run into each other for the rest of our lives, continuing a sort of close intimate bond, but then I'm sort of—how do you say—amorous. So I don't think I could ever be in a monogamous, marriage-type arrangement. I could get married to somebody, but it wouldn't be emotionally exclusive. Shit, I'd have to process for a few years to figure this out.

I want to have more of a community, a roving community of friends, which is sort of what I created for myself anyway. A community of people whom I feel very close to, that I sort of consider a family, which I kind of have now with my housemates. I have people with whom I feel very close, and that sort of constitutes a family for me; that's kind of what I define as a family. I'd like to have a stable place where all of the people that I care about were sort of in a little community together. But you never know. For all I know, the world could end tomorrow and none of this happens.

I plan on making my queer identity a large part of my life. I'm not going to be a professional lesbian, but I'm gonna be a professional activist, and a lot of that's going to be stopping the existence of homophobia. I'm sort of a raving ecofeminist, you might say. And so, I'm just working toward the attainment of a more humanitarian culture. That's sort of what I intend to do. I'm as out as out can be and want to continue being really out. I tell everyone; that's why I'm using my real name here.

Paige

My professional goal is probably getting a double major, political science, gay/lesbian studies, women's studies, something like that, and then to law school. Child advocacy is where I'm heading right now, this week. I'd like to live in California. That's my goal. I'd really like to live in the Santa Cruz Mountains; I love it up there. A normal life, you know. I don't know if that's too much to ask, but nothing extraordinarily exotic. I want to fall in love and be happy. I really love kids, but I don't know. I definitely see it as an option to have kids. I don't see anything blocking me from doing that. But I don't know. We'll see.

I see my identity as a lesbian influencing life. I'd like to bring it into wider acceptance, and not just have lesbian friends and just have straight friends and just have gay friends. I think a nice meld of all my groups of friends would be great.

Eventually, in my life, later on, I'd like to set up some type of community housing group where I provide not only legal assistance for gay youth, but also housing and support and counseling. That's one of my goals for later on. It's not going to happen anytime soon unless I run into about $6 million. But that's what I'm looking for in my future—set up some type of support network. Because I think I definitely could have used more of that. I think everyone could have used more of it. Someplace where they know they can go and spend the night or whatever and be safe.

Todd Fay-Long

I'm seventeen; I'm in college; I'm moving out. I just feel like I'm much more together than most of the people my age, or most of my friends that are my age. The gay people I know who are my age whom I have a lot in common with are active in the gay community and really working for change. The people who aren't in our youth group are just more like, "Oh, let's party all the time."

We're starting a youth group in Petaluma now, because this guy named Robin, who was fifteen, committed suicide a couple months ago; he jumped off the Golden Gate Bridge. He was gay. I went out with him a couple of times. He went to Petaluma High, and there's no youth group in Petaluma. There's a Sonoma County youth group, but it's all the way in Santa Rosa, and that's a half hour away, and if you don't have a car, it's hard to get there. So I'm really excited about that; it's been a dream of mine to start a support group ever since I went to school there. That's where my passion is right now.

But also, I've gotten a little bit burnt out on being all activist. For a while, I was going to four gay rights meetings a week, just being so involved, and everything I'd write about in school would be about gay rights. I'm just kinda burnt out. But I think a lot of people do that when they first come out. They totally wear their freedom rings and just act really gay and want to do everything gay, gay, gay. And I'm kinda burnt out on that.

I'm just really into the rave scene and have friends from there. I'm gay; I'm comfortable with it. I don't need to be around all gay people anymore, 'cause I can be comfortable around other people. But I'm still involved, as far as activism and that kind of thing.

I really want to go to Harvey Milk Institute, an all gay and lesbian studies school in San Francisco, because the school I go to now has no gay and lesbian history classes or anything like that. It would be nice if there was a class, but there's not, and I want to learn about gay history.

I'm really interested in the 1970s and what happened in the 1970s, as far as gay culture. That's when the gay culture really seemed to start. There was Stonewall, and it started before then, but it was in the 1970s that it was becoming acceptable, and that's when all the discos started and that kinda thing. I'm really interested in that, and I'm interested in that lifestyle that changed.

In the 1970s people had sex a lot because there was no AIDS, and I'm really interested in the pre-AIDS era. I want to study that. Our community was really self-destructive in the 1970s. And it still is in a lot of ways. Like in the Castro, the same kind of people who were around in the 1970s are still there. A lot of the young gay people I know who party all the time, they're just the same as people were in the 1970s; they don't take care of themselves. I'm worried, because I know that a lot of them are gonna get AIDS because they just have sex all the time, and you can't do that.

I consider myself more promiscuous than I'd like to be, but not as promiscuous, not nearly as promiscuous, as most guys out there. I would never have sex with somebody whom I didn't want to have sex with and whom I wasn't attracted to, but a lot of people do. They feel loved when they have sex, and they want to make up for all the hate that they experienced. Especially in school.

I want my major to be gender studies and how it relates to English. If I get a degree in that, you can't really do anything else but teach. I'll probably end up teaching. Then sometimes I just don't think I even want a serious job. Sometimes I think I just want to be a dancer or a hairdresser or something. I just think it would be easier to have some regular job and be able to go dancing and stuff like that. But then I just think I want to make something out of my life, and I don't want to just be some generic person.

I go to a lot of raves, and I really want to be involved with putting those together. I'm starting to get involved with this one rave, and

I'm going to start helping set up and get their sound system and stuff like that. So who knows what I'll end up doing in my life.

I want to move to San Francisco. I don't want to live in the Castro though. It may be fun for a couple months, but I would get tired of it. I don't want to have to look that cute every day. I just don't have the energy to be all sprayed and coiffed like that every day.

Jim

I want to do something helping people with AIDS, like counseling and stuff. I think it's really important. I want to do art—ceramics, sculptures; I like drawing with colored pencil a lot, for some reason. And I like drawing the human body a lot too. I don't know if I'll ever get married or have kids. I definitely won't have kids. I hate kids. I can't stand kids. If I loved somebody enough, I'd get married. But I don't think I'd have kids. If I was in love with the person I met, I would want to get legally married.

Chapter 12

Listen Up! Messages to Others

Anthony Gomez

All I've gotta say is, "What's the use in hassling kids like me? Is this some kind of way to pick up your own ego, or something like that?" I have so many questions for people who pick on people like me. Okay, you call me this because?. . .Your point by calling me this is?. . . I think before they clean up anybody else's backyard, they need to clean up their own first.

I think what needs to be done is to have more classes about all this, in health or sex ed. Right now, in sex ed, the teachers don't tell you about being gay or anything having to do with gays, only that things have to be straight. I think they should expand their horizons on that, adding some gay literature for kids to understand. And I think the parents should do this reading as well. I don't think it's wrong to be gay; I like who I am. I'm a queen, and that is peachy keen with me. I am a flame, and that is okay! Society needs to stop putting all this emphasis and ridicule on gays—"They're sick; they're unnatural."

I think straight people should accept gay views. No matter if they like it or not, we're still gonna be here. When they die and they're all crippled, we're gonna be here. And they better start accepting us now before it's too late. Teachers have to know how to accept students for being gay or being different, because different is good. I think the parents should go out there and teach their kids that this is okay. Just because somebody's different from you doesn't mean you have to back away.

I've been hospitalized for suicide attempts five times, last time I counted. One time I tried measuring my life with sleeping pills. Counting, "This one's for living, this one's for dying, this one's for living." I found twenty-nine reasons to die, and I found around eleven reasons to live. I think society should stop saying that gays are so bad and it's not right to be gay and all this stuff. It's not true. We don't go out there saying that their sexual preference is wrong.

I would also say to the gay kids reading this that everybody has a different time span. If you think you're gay, read books about what that means, go explore what the gay community is like. I'm not saying have sex. I'm saying read books, go places, and just take it one step at a time. When you're ready for one step, go to the next step. Don't try to do it all at once.

Eileene Coscolluela

Please be there for the kids, the questioning youth, the youth who have come out. That is so important. Having an adult stand by you is a powerful thing. Having a peer stand by you is even more powerful. Be there. Be out or an ally.

Dawn McCausland

I don't find support from the older gay community. I don't mean to be attacking here, but they almost have the same perspective as a lot of the straight adults do: gay youth really don't exist or have needs. They don't really recognize that they could be really influential in a young gay kid's life. They don't really realize that there's gay youth groups around or that they could volunteer or that they could give money or that they could be a role model for a kid. It's frustrating. We do a mentoring program in the youth group I'm in, where the youth are set up with screened gay adults so that we can have almost a role model situation. It meant a lot to be able to take my girlfriend and her mentor's lover to meet my mentor and her wife and have this group dinner and see what a lesbian house "looks like," and see how they interact and how they greet each other, and it was just like, "Oh, I want to do this when I'm older."

We always talk about so much of the negative stuff or the hard times and the coming out and the self-hate and internalized homophobia and all that shit that we go through. But we never talk that much about the fun stuff. It's horrible to come out, in a lot of ways, and to deal with it. There's so many times where I was sitting there just going, "Why am I feeling this way, and goddamn it, I don't want to be this way; I don't want to do this." I wanted to change so many times. But I also knew that I wasn't going to oppress myself. I wasn't going to keep down or suppress anything in me. I fought it, and then I just said, "Well, fuck it, this is you, and you're gonna be you, no matter what." The first time joining the group was scary, and there was the big white light in my face, and I don't remember anything, and I was freaked out to hell. All my homophobia's coming up, and my biphobia and all this shit and all my fear. Girls are looking at me, and I'm thinking, "I've never had sex with a girl; what am I gonna do?" But after that, there's all the fun stuff. There's going into the coffee shops and being out, and sitting at a table with straight people, bi people, gay men, and lesbians, and sitting there and scamming on people. And going, "There's a cute girl; if she's straight, she's yours; if she's gay, she's mine."

Stuff can be fun. I embrace the term "dyke." My friends embrace the term "fag." It's not that that's inherently bad. It's just that the social stigma of the dyke implies someone who doesn't conform to traditional gender roles. When I was called a dyke it was because of the way I looked or when I was doing a lesbian activity. But there's nothing inherently bad about being a dyke once you accept being gay. So it was like, "Yeah, fuck, I'm a dyke, and that's righteous," "I look like a dyke; I act like a dyke; I talk like a dyke, I'm dating a dyke." That's who we are, and it's just that they don't like it that makes it bad.

Once you get in a community and you get into a group of friends and you take your trips to the Castro and you go into your first gay bookstore and you walk down the street, it's like, "I'm in a gay Disneyland, and everyone's gay!" This is what everybody else feels like in society. You know what I mean? Everything is identified for them.

People joke that I could see a pride flag from a mile away. Fuck, I see pride flags in Safeway ads. I see pink triangles just in regular graphic design. Instant family, wherever you go. You just give them this look or this smile or this wave, saying that you're the same.

We go to a place, and we will define the party. We will make it; we will make a party anywhere we are at any time. We are the loudest, the funniest. We just feel comfortable and very happy together. You go to a coffee shop and you just own the place. If someone's homophobic, then they're gonna leave before you will. You're not gonna shut up for anybody else. There's so much freedom in that. On a serious note, I'm feeling real preachy here, but don't forget that you can get AIDS from lesbian sex. Otherwise, just fuckin' go for it; be yourself—be a butch, be a femme, be a dyke.

Eriq Chang

Oh, god. Be yourself; look at your situation and how safe it is. Because, I don't think our society, the whole world, will ever be able to accept one thing; everybody is gonna have their own opinion. I guess I really don't think you can actually gain 100 percent equality. Just as it is with blacks. Everybody has their opinion, and you have to be yourself and make it work for yourself. If you're yourself, and you portray a positive image, people aren't gonna look at your sexual identity. They're gonna look at this vibe you have. I've been able to do that. People look at me and don't look at, "Omigod, Eriq, you like guys *and* girls. . . ." I definitely would say, don't lie. Don't lie to yourself especially. If you're attracted to something, that's natural and that's not a burden; it's not something that's a curse. I don't think it's abnormal. I think that you've got something special. It's what makes everybody individual. Go along your own karmic wheel and reach nirvana your own way. Be yourself, and that will get you what you want.

Ernie Hsiung

You're not alone in the world. I thought I was. I learned in college that a lot of other people thought they were, too. But we're not alone.

Kyallee Santanders

I was a lucky one—I had a friend to talk to, and I found a support group. Most gay teens do not have these luxuries. We grow up hating ourselves like society teaches us to. I would not be here today if I had succeeded in my suicide attempt. If someone would've been "out" at my school—if the teachers wouldn't have been afraid to stop the "fag" and "dyke" jokes, if my human sexuality class had even mentioned homosexuality (especially in a positive light), if the school counselors would have been open to discussion of gay and lesbian issues, perhaps I wouldn't have grown up hating what I was and perhaps I wouldn't have attempted suicide.

I tried to die and failed. Many of my peers have succeeded. We have the ability to make this lunacy stop. If you're gay or lesbian or bisexual or transgendered, come out and let the youth know that you exist. Be a role model. If you're a teacher, don't tolerate the "fag" and "dyke" jokes—they hurt us and drive us farther into the closet. Acknowledge the accomplishments of gays and lesbians in history too—we have been here all along and surely our contributions count for something. And if you're just the average person doing your average thing, don't tolerate the hatred and lies. Put yourself in our shoes—it's a pretty crummy place to be with today's political atmosphere. Don't buy into the stereotypes. Learn the truth about who gays and lesbians are and share this truth with others. Thirty percent of teen suicides are committed by gay teens, and we only number one in ten. It's time to stop the madness.

Lisa Campbell

Well, having an out teacher helps at school. At my school, we had Bob Latham who was out. We had other teachers rumored about, and some people I know for a fact were gay, but no one else was out. I think one other teacher's gonna come out this year. Bob retired, and this teacher's taking over the gay youth group at school. I've known her for quite a while. Having out teachers, having out students, having the administration not let derogatory comments toward gays, or any race, go unnoticed, that would really help. And just making sure there are punishments for that would help a lot.

I'd say to the straight community that they need to lighten up; they need to really take a look at who we are, get to know somebody who is queer, and then see how normal and sometimes boring our lives can be. For people who are gay, you don't have to flaunt who you are to get accepted. I'm not gonna say don't flaunt who you are. Be happy, be merry, live life to the fullest. Also, just remember, the queer community needs to focus on its youth so that we have more adults in the future who can help us out politically. The more of us there are, the less of them there are out there to work against us.

The community can't be unified if it doesn't know one another. If you have young people who know their elders, then we can see their interests as well as them seeing ours. Different age groups have different interests. There needs to be more of a link between the two groups to see other things, other directions, so that we move in a uniform direction. There's a lot of split places in our community. There's the leather community, there's youth, there's the Berkeleyite lesbian separatists—all these diverse people who need to just know one another so that they can see one another's issues. But there need to be more things where people can see one another's issues and kinda figure out where they are coming from.

Books help that out, and people seeing one another at community centers and stuff, going places with an open mind. We are all supposed to be so open and have such open minds, but a lot of people don't. Even if you're gay, it doesn't mean you have an open mind. You may not be open to this one other person's experience or lifestyle, but you've got to let others tell you their stories, get some knowledge about it before you make a judgment.

Others have just as much of a right to live their lives the way they want to as I have the right to live my life the way I want to. My mom raised me with a pretty open mind about other cultures and stuff. I was pretty open-minded about a lot of different things; however, I knew there were limits. There were things that you weren't supposed to be; you weren't supposed to be lesbian, none of those things. Queer was not what you were supposed to be. But, with the way that I was raised, I was open to other people's experiences. That's how I get people to accept me.

I won the Bobbie Griffith's Memorial Scholarship Award. What won me that was one sentence, I think. What I put at the end was that I thought that the gay community wasn't gonna get anywhere in Congress the way it was right now, with all the Republicans there. And I said that basically our focus for the time being should be on youth and getting the suicide rate down. You get the suicide rate down, you get more gay adults, okay. You get more gay voters in the future. And then, you'll get what you want.

Michael Talis

Before you act on anything, talk to someone else who is a homosexual. Try to understand better how you feel about everything before you get involved with outsiders. If you can't find someone to talk with, read books or watch movies about homosexuality. It helps. When you're feeling down and out because of your gayness, just remember that there's a million other people out there with your problems. Find them and talk with them. You'll feel better.

Mary Toth

I want to tell other youth not to kill themselves, because that's something I came very close to doing. Especially for kids who are somewhat—I don't know if eccentric would be quite the word—but kids who don't fit in anyway—what a hard road it is! If you already don't fit in *and* you're a queer, it can be a real uphill battle. But there is a light at the end of the tunnel, and no, it's not an oncoming train.

It's easier to form an identity of yourself that you determine. Being self-determined is much easier in the gay and lesbian community because there's a lot more acceptance of it. Every lesbian I know is out there trying to find herself. Oh, shit, it's not like there are limited options. So the queer community can be a lot more accepting of your difference. Ideally, I want more of a cohesive community, so that there could be more of that kind of support for odd girls and everyone.

Paige

I really think awareness needs to be promoted and tied in with education, where we have a little bit of AIDS education, a little bit of sex education. I definitely think there should be some lifestyles education. Maybe even a slight bit of sensitivity training. And I know in Morgan Hill, my hometown, the high school has an excellent gay/lesbian/bisexual support group that is sponsored by a teacher at school. Ideally I'd love to see all those things. I don't see why it can't happen, but I know it's not gonna happen anytime soon—at least in my school. The administration that's there is very old school, and they're not dead yet. And until they die, there won't be any fresh people that come through. Ted—the principal—the guy is seventy years old—he wears hearing aids in both ears; you have to yell at him to get his attention! We have very few young teachers, and in order to get a more upbeat feeling in the school, we need to have some young teachers and some young blood.

And parents: Make it more available for your kids to come to you and say, "I'm a lesbian." Just be more open-minded; put more things out there for youth.

Jim

I think older people see being bisexual as a trend really. They call it a phase, and I think that's so dumb. Just because they weren't as open as we are now. I think it's so cool that most people have just accepted us and what we're about. In the past couple years, it's just gotten better, and I think it will just keep getting better. There's always going to be that small, hopefully small, percentage against us, but it's one of my dreams that it will just keep getting smaller.

I think that whatever makes whoever it is happy, they should pursue it, and I think they should do whatever they want as long as it makes them happy. You have to be selfish in life. You have to do what you want to do. I'm not really scared of just anybody finding out. I'm just scared of the rejection. I don't want anyone to reject me, but if they do, then that's something I have to deal with. Life goes on.